Dr. Betsy Altmaier has produced an exceptional and sensitive book specifically for survivors of child sexual abuse. She offers information about her own abuse experience, coupled with sound psychological information about what it takes to leave the darkness of sexual abuse behind and to live life forward. Her information is hopeful and encourages the view of recovery as a process that requires perseverance over time. Her suggested readings and exercises are "on point" and support the recovery process in a very practical way. Highly recommended!

—CHRISTINE A. COURTOIS, PHD, ABPP, LICENSED PSYCHOLOGIST AND AUTHOR OF *HEALING THE INCEST WOUND: ADULT SURVIVORS IN THERAPY* AND *IT'S NOT YOU, IT'S WHAT HAPPENED TO YOU: COMPLEX TRAUMA AND TREATMENT*

This informative book brings a combination of new research, insights, and strategies to help survivors of child sexual abuse. It offers the resources and strategies survivors will need at different points in their recovery. The author offers both the expertise of a seasoned therapist and researcher, and the empathy and deep understanding of someone who is a survivor herself—a combination that will no doubt engender both trust and encouragement.

—BEVERLY ENGEL, LMFT, PSYCHOTHERAPIST, LOS OSOS, CA

LEAVING DARKNESS BEHIND

ELIZABETH M. ALTMAIER, PHD

LEAVING DARKNESS BEHIND

RECOVERY *from*
CHILDHOOD SEXUAL ABUSE

 AMERICAN PSYCHOLOGICAL ASSOCIATION

Published by
American Psychological Association
750 First Street, NE
Washington, DC 20002
https://www.apa.org

Order Department
https://www.apa.org/pubs/books
order@apa.org

In the U.K., Europe, Africa, and the Middle East, copies may be ordered from
Eurospan
https://www.eurospanbookstore.com/apa
info@eurospangroup.com

Typeset in Sabon by Circle Graphics, Inc., Reisterstown, MD

Printer: Gasch Printing, Odenton, MD
Cover Designer: Mark Karis

Library of Congress Cataloging-in-Publication Data

Names: Altmaier, Elizabeth M., author.
Title: Leaving darkness behind : recovery from childhood sexual abuse /
    by Elizabeth M. Altmaier.
Description: Washington, DC : American Psychological Association, [2021] |
    Includes bibliographical references and index.
Identifiers: LCCN 2021013021 (print) | LCCN 2021013022 (ebook) |
    ISBN 9781433833939 (paperback) | ISBN 9781433838293 (ebook)
Subjects: LCSH: Sexual abuse victims—Rehabilitation.
Classification: LCC RC560.S44 A83 2021 (print) | LCC RC560.S44 (ebook) |
    DDC 362.76/4—dc23
LC record available at https://lccn.loc.gov/2021013021
LC ebook record available at https://lccn.loc.gov/2021013022

https://doi.org/10.1037/0000265-000

Printed in the United States of America

10 9 8 7 6 5 4 3 2 1

CONTENTS

Contents

ACKNOWLEDGMENTS

About 5 years ago, as I was finishing the first of what became a series of books on trauma and its healing, I concluded that books are birthed through a painful process centered on the author. This author is fortunately sustained by a team of companions. I am even more indebted to my team for their support of this book for survivors.

At the American Psychological Association, I benefited from the steady guidance of Emily Ekle and Susan Herman. I also thank my three reviewers for their thoughtful critique and many excellent suggestions.

I thank the many authors whose work succeeded in conveying difficult truths about childhood sexual abuse, and those clinicians and scholars who have helped create the knowledge we have now about complex trauma and its treatment.

And I thank my specific companions on this segment of my journey—Lydia, Ben, and Kimberly. You are truly with me on the path.

LEAVING DARKNESS BEHIND

DEFINING RECOVERY

If you are reading this book, then you know it is written for adults who were sexually abused as children. Whether you are a survivor, or you care about a survivor, or you are interested in learning more about childhood sexual abuse, this book will help you. In it, I share information about childhood sexual abuse, including facts about its occurrence and its consequences for survivors. I am a psychologist who translates scientific findings so that nonpsychologists can understand them. Researchers in my field have published thousands of studies on childhood sexual abuse, most of which were published in the past several decades. This book rests on that research.

It also describes positive processes, called "strengths," that survivors can work on to help in their recovery. Although you have likely recognized all kinds of personal strengths in others or in yourself over the years, a movement known as "positive psychology" has reinvigorated interest in strengths and has provided new scholarship about them. Strengths have been demonstrated to be useful to individuals as they confront challenges, and even traumatic events. Chapters 4 through 11 will help you learn about strengths and increase your use of them.

But more than conveying information, my goal in this book is to help survivors leave their darkness behind. If you are a survivor, you know what I mean when I say "darkness." Because I am a survivor of childhood sexual abuse myself, darkness is something I have felt in many ways over many years. Darkness is waking up and being disappointed you are still alive. Darkness is seeing evil inside a person who is supposed to love and care for you. Darkness is being so caught up in your thoughts and feelings that you cannot escape them. Darkness is living in the prison of your memories. Darkness is seeing yourself as bad, wrong, dirty, contaminated, and shameful. But it is possible to leave that darkness behind and to recover from its effects on your physical and mental health and your life.

Leaving the darkness behind does not mean erasing painful memories. Recovering is not the same as forgetting. Neither is it sanitizing our memories of what happened to us, or somehow making the actions of others acceptable. Darkness is overcome only by shining a light on it. We shine a light on our darkness by using certain thoughts, emotions, actions, and practices to accept those memories for what they were and to use them to energize a new, healthy life. Trauma survivors who have left and are leaving behind the darkness are not happy all the time. But they continue to actively build their own recovery through the strengths I elaborate on in Chapters 4 through 11.

It is not possible for you to throw a switch and change suddenly from darkness to light. Do not believe anyone who tells you that this or that can accomplish that goal. Rather, recovery is a painful and difficult journey—a series of paths you walk along toward a destination. One of the earliest pictures that helped me visualize my journey was a pathway leaving a dark forest and joining a meadow in the sunlight with flowers and birds and a bench to sit on and think. It is great for you to have pictures of your recovery; you can collect them online, draw or paint them yourself, or use any other method to record them.

As you read this book, you'll find out about different practices you can adopt to help you. For example, one day you are feeling sluggish and on the brink of tears for no apparent reason. Because you have learned about grief in Chapter 5, you recognize those signals as meaning that you need to grieve. So you use strategies and strengths to allow that grief to be fully experienced and to help you grow. Many of the chapters in this book deal with emotions because they are difficult companions for us. At this point on your recovery path, you will find that some strategies and strengths work for you now, and in the future you will find that others are a better match.

How is this book different from a self-help workbook? One way is that you will learn more about the science behind strengths and strategies. Understanding that content may take effort, more so than trying out an exercise. But I believe that understanding the science will help you adopt the strategies in the full knowledge of their meaning and intended effect. Although this book is not a self-help workbook, I do list many of those in the Resources section at the end of each chapter because those workbooks go into more detail on exercises than I can here.

I should note that I cannot cover every possible situation survivors face. An example is the difficult situation of confronting your abuser or disclosing your abuse. That choice gives most survivors great distress because there doesn't seem to be a "right" decision. Disclosure of abuse creates terrible tension in families and can result in the survivor being shunned or their experience denied. But holding the information in, especially if you are in contact with the abuser or that person is in your family, is equally terrible. This decision is a central barrier to survivors' growth and healing. Again, I list workbooks and resources that can be helpful to you, although I cannot give you a step-by-step guide to decision making.

Ultimately, you will create a portfolio for thriving. This portfolio may have tangible aspects, such as journals, pictures, photos, audio recordings, and so on. When I speak of a "portfolio," I am referring to a collection of resources you can access and strengths that exist within you to meet the challenges you face. As you develop these resources and identify and build your strengths, you will put them to work for you at different points in your recovery journey.

WHAT IS IN THIS BOOK?

The first two chapters of this book provide foundational information on childhood sexual abuse. Chapter 1 includes facts about its occurrence and effects in childhood and adulthood. It also discusses and corrects misbeliefs about childhood sexual abuse. In Chapter 2, I examine the concept of complex trauma, which can be a helpful way to understand your present situation.

Chapter 3 explains recovery, setting it as the bridge between the information about childhood sexual abuse (Chapters 1 and 2) and the resources provided by the strengths of resilience, grief, meaning, spirituality, connection, forgiveness, and hope. Chapters 4 through 10 each focuses on a strength, providing information about that strength and exercises called "self-assessments" to help you apply the information to yourself. The final chapter, Chapter 11, ties all this content together in the concept of thriving and describes how to create a strengths portfolio for yourself.

All chapters include several features. Recovery Milestones list the important points covered in each chapter. Self-Assessments are exercises you can use to learn about you. Insights From Psychology present the results of a research project that is especially relevant to the chapter. And each chapter ends with a list of resources for additional reading or exercises and self-assessments. If you wish to read further regarding a specific research study covered in a chapter, you can locate it using the reference list at the end of the book.

You may be a journaling person. I know that I was not. But I encourage you to try journaling as you read this book. There are many places in the chapters where you are prompted to write out a response. Even if you have not journaled in the past, treat yourself to a real (paper) journal, or get your favorite note-taking app ready. One of my dear friends, a survivor herself, was so committed to getting me to journal that she kept giving me differently formatted journals! I am finally getting more comfortable with that process and can see its benefits, and I'm sure you will, too.

I also encourage you to use this book in a way that best suits you. That may be to start at the beginning and end at the end. But you can also start with any topic that interests you and cover the chapters in any order. If previous content might be necessary to understand something in a chapter, I provide a brief summary of that content so you don't have to read the previous chapter until you're ready.

I also use headings intentionally to alert you to the content and help you avoid being triggered. If "triggered" is a new word to you, to be *triggered* is to experience sudden, intense feelings and reactions to a situation or a person—essentially, to experience a trauma all over again. This is more than something rubbing you the wrong way. Being triggered is a frightening reexperience of the original trauma. If you feel triggered, you can move away from the content, calm yourself down with deep breathing and visual imagery, and set the book down until you feel ready to pick it up again.

My goal for this book is to help you use information and tools to envision and enact strategies that are unique to you and your strengths and that help you move you ahead in your recovery journey. I have a more personal call to you below.

MY PLEDGE TO YOU

Dear Reader,

It is common to begin a book with an Introduction, as I have done here. That section of a book is the author's way of talking directly to you and explaining what they are hoping you will learn as you read the book. But you are in my mind much more often than in a single chapter. Because of the pandemic, I am working from home, and my dining room is my new office. My table holds stacks of books and papers, and my chairs are filing drawer cabinets. And you sit across the table from me. I hear your voice, see your tears, witness your suffering. That was not true of my office on the university campus, where I usually work. So it is a good thing we were brought here to be together.

Here is what I pledge to you about this book:

First, I will do everything I can do as the author to help you feel safe. There is a lot of content in this book that is "dark." And in fact, one person who read an earlier draft thought there was too much darkness. But I know, as a survivor myself, that there can never be too much darkness if I am going to tell the truth. Still, you also need to protect yourself. So each chapter has a capsule summary at the beginning showing what is covered in that chapter, and there are headings to help you decide what you might want to read and what you might want to skip and perhaps come back to later.

Second, you will understand yourself. It is liberating, truly, to know that what you are experiencing is not because you are bad or evil or seductive or stupid or dirty. You are experiencing the natural and even inevitable results of what happened *to you*. You were a *victim*. You are *not at fault*, no matter who said what to you then or now.

Three, you will have accurate labels for your experiences, thoughts, feelings, symptoms, problems, and the like. When I hear you use terms like "self-compassion," "betrayal trauma," and "broaden and build," I will be smiling. You will have become an expert on yourself. Here is my parallel: If you were to be diagnosed with cancer, you would know the name of it, you would learn how it affects your body, and you would have the terms for the treatments you receive. This situation—your situation—is no different.

Fourth, you will learn. *A lot.* You will learn about childhood sexual abuse, about complex trauma, about recovery, and about strengths that will help you along your recovery journey—resilience, grief, meaning, spirituality, connection, forgiveness, and hope. You will also learn about thriving. If you find the content to be difficult, you may need to pick the book up, read a bit, and set it down, or it may help to read it while you are doing something else. That is all right. Or you may find that the content demands all of your attention, that you can't read it over coffee, for example, while also binging your favorite show. Again, how you are best able to learn and apply the content is the best way for you to read it.

Fifth, you will get to know me a bit. This book is not a memoir, and my story is not your story. But I am a victim, and I am a survivor, and on my best days I am a thriver. Some of that comes through.

Dear reader, we share a bond that is unbreakable. It was forged in terrible darkness. The chains hold us down. But I want you to know that this situation is not permanent, and that you can become the author of a new story, the story of your recovery. It is an honor for me to be with you for part of that new story.

CHAPTER I

CHILDHOOD SEXUAL ABUSE: YOU ARE NOT ALONE

Recovery Milestones

This chapter will help you

1. **learn** correct information about childhood sexual abuse;
2. **examine** how childhood sexual abuse causes damage in childhood that persists into adulthood; and
3. **describe** three types of damage from childhood sexual abuse—damage to your body, to your mind, and to your emotions.

As I wrote this book, the media was overflowing with coverage of sexual abuse of children and adolescents. For example, Larry Nassar, a physician at Michigan State University and doctor for USA Gymnastics, was convicted of sexual abuse in 2018. At his sentencing hearing, he was confronted by more than 150 women he had abused as children or adolescents. Their deeply emotional testimony extended over 7 days and was witnessed or read by many. The first victim to testify told of her abuse; starting when she was 6, Nassar exposed himself to her, then masturbated in front of her, and finally physically abused her. When she told her parents, and they asked him about it, he denied it. Her disbelieving parents urged her to apologize to him.

If you are reading this book, you, or someone you love, was a victim of sexual abuse during childhood or adolescence. Generally, victims feel isolated in this experience for several reasons. There is public coverage of the topic, but not in a way that helps a particular victim. Victims feel shame and fear and cannot talk to another person about it. And abuse creates ambiguity and disbelief even within victims, so they call their own experience into question. Therefore, my goal in this chapter is to provide information and support for you.

This chapter presents information on childhood sexual abuse, including what it is, how often it occurs, and what is wrongly believed about it. I describe what psychologists know about its effects. I explain both immediate and long-term consequences of experiencing childhood sexual abuse. I use chapter headings carefully so you can read sections you feel comfortable reading and return to uncomfortable sections when you are able. As I explained in the Introduction, you should feel safe reading this book, and you should intentionally select what you want to read and in what order.

In learning about childhood sexual abuse as you read this book, you will see both the term "victim" and the term "survivor." Mental health professionals prefer the term "survivor" because it implies empowerment after the trauma. But the term "victim" also is used in this book, to mean that the survivor of childhood sexual abuse actually was a victim who was attacked and brutalized. Because doubt sometimes exists, there must be acceptance that people who experienced abuse were not at fault, could not defend themselves, and were truly victims.

WHAT IS CHILDHOOD SEXUAL ABUSE?

Child abuse happens when the *perpetrator*, the person who is the abuser, intentionally harms a *minor victim*, a person under age 18. There are four types of child abuse: physical abuse, neglect, emotional abuse, and sexual abuse. *Physical abuse* is nonaccidental physical injury inflicted on the child causing injuries ranging from bruises to burns to fractures to death. *Neglect* is failure of a parent or caregiver to provide for the child's needs for shelter, nutrition, supervision, and medical care. *Emotional abuse* occurs when the perpetrator interacts with the child in ways that injure the child's normal emotional development; examples include constant criticism and belittling, such as saying, "I wish you had never been born." Some states also identify parental substance abuse as child abuse; when a parent is abusing substances, it damages their ability to parent, often resulting in neglect of the child.

Childhood sexual abuse is a specific form of child abuse in which the child is used for the sexual stimulation of the perpetrator or an observer and to meet adult desires; the abuse may occur once, or a few times, or over several years. For some perpetrators, the desires are erotic in nature; a person with a sexual preference for children is a *pedophile*. Pedophiles may not have sexual relations exclusively with children; they may be married or have sexual relations with adults. Other perpetrators have normal nonsexual desires—such as for physical closeness or for control or for affection—that become the motivation for sexual behaviors.

Whatever the motive behind sexual abuse, it is always without consent. Sometimes perpetrators claim that the child agreed to the sexual behaviors or "wanted it." But a child cannot truly consent because of the child's age, or because of the relationship the child has with the perpetrator, or because the child is emotionally attached to the perpetrator. This inability to consent is also true when the child is an older child or adolescent and the perpetrator claims the sexual interaction was consensual. Even for older children, there is still a power difference, or a physical strength discrepancy, or an emotional dependence.

CORRECTING WRONGFUL BELIEFS ABOUT CHILDHOOD SEXUAL ABUSE

There are many beliefs about childhood sexual abuse that are wrong. Some of these beliefs persist because they reduce the fear that parents have about the possibility that their child will experience abuse. Others persist because of a lack of familiarity with facts from research. The bulleted statements that follow are facts that correct beliefs that are often wrongly held.

- Childhood sexual abuse can involve not touching as well as penetration ("rape") or other forms of touching.
- It is wrong to believe that sexual abuse is only genital penetration, either vaginal or anal.

Abuse may involve touching; an example is when a child is fondled during a bath or playtime. Another example is when a child is enticed or forced to perform a sex act on the perpetrator.

Abuse may also not involve touching. An example is when a child poses for sexually explicit photos or is forced to watch pornography. Another example is when the perpetrator tries to look at a child's naked body or masturbates while watching the child. The interaction can also be digital, as when a child is forced to send or receive pictures or texts that are sexual in nature.

- Childhood sexual abuse is never provoked by the child.
- It is wrong to believe that childhood sexual abuse is provoked by the child.

Children are not developmentally able to understand the true nature of sexual behaviors. They may believe the perpetrator's assertions that these interactions show normal caring for the child. They may be told they are loved, but the sexual contact is confusing and unwanted. They may feel pain but are told that they "liked it." But children never provoke their own abuse.

- Childhood sexual abuse cannot be stopped by the child.
- It is wrong to believe that the child could have ended the abuse by escaping or by saying "stop."

The reason the interactions are abusive is that they are forced on the child, either literally or symbolically. A child may be dependent on the perpetrator, as occurs in families. A child may be emotionally attached to the perpetrator, as occurs in social contexts, such as a sports team the perpetrator coaches. A child may be in a powerless position, as occurs in contexts involving a youth pastor or a camp counselor. Children may also be coerced by threats designed to make them feel guilty or scared, for example, that reporting abuse could lead to the perpetrator's going to jail or to the breakup of the family.

- Only 10% of abuse is caused by a person unknown to the child; the rest is abuse by family members or adults known to the child.
- It is wrong to believe that in all cases of abuse, the perpetrator is a stranger who finds the child alone in an isolated location or kidnaps the child.

Starting in the late 1970s, media coverage increased of crimes in which a child was abducted and killed, and the idea of "stranger danger" was circulated. Children were taught not to talk to people they did not know and not to get into a car or van with a stranger. The reality, however, is that 90% of abused children know their abuser; family and extended family are about half of this group, and acquaintances of the family and children are the other half. Strangers are the smallest group, about 10% (Townsend et al., 2016).

- Childhood sexual abuse is not unusual or rare; it is actually common.
- It is wrong to believe that childhood sexual abuse is uncommon or rare (see Douglas & Finkelhor, 2005).

Statistics about the occurrence of child sexual abuse include "incidence" and "prevalence." *Incidence* is the number of new cases in a given time period, such as a year, reported by official agencies, such as child welfare organizations, or by children themselves through survey research. Incidence data from law enforcement agencies reveal that between 1.2 and 1.9 children per 1,000 are abused in a single year, and incidence data from children and teenagers reveal a range of 4 to 32 per 1,000. The incidence for older children is the same as that of new cases of breast cancer for women, a life event we might consider relatively frequent. *Prevalence* is the number of adults who report having experienced childhood sexual abuse at any time before age 18. Prevalence data reveal that 12% to 30% of adults report experiencing sexual abuse during childhood. There are gender differences in that range; women report a higher prevalence (17%–30%) than do men (7%–13%; Douglas & Finkelhor, 2005).

- Although false accusations are sometimes made, they are very rare; if a child makes an accusation of abuse, it should be treated as truthful.
- It is wrong to believe that many accusations of abuse are false.

An argument about false accusations and a related topic, false memory, took place among psychologists in the 1990s. But research on this topic has determined that very few allegations—only about 2%—were later determined to be false (O'Donohue et al., 2018). Data also show that most children never tell another person about the abuse (Winters et al., 2020). They fear being punished or ostracized. They fear that someone they know or love could go to jail. They fear not being believed. They fear being blamed for the abuse. Responses such as "He didn't do that to you," "Why didn't you tell me?" and "Why didn't you just say no?" are often what greet a child's disclosure.

- Childhood sexual abuse usually happens without anyone knowing.
- It is wrong to believe that someone would "know" if it was happening.

Parents say, "I would know if my child was being abused." Teachers say, "I would know if a child in my classroom was being abused at home." Because we believe that abusers are bad and can be recognized as bad, that belief lets us continue to rely on our own lack of ability to recognize abuse. We "fool ourselves we aren't being fooled" (Freyd & Birrell, 2013).

- Childhood sexual abuse occurs in virtually every setting in which children are placed.
- It is wrong to believe that childhood sexual abuse simply does not occur in certain settings.

A prime example of where people do not believe abuse can occur is a setting motivated by religion, such as a church, youth group, summer camp, or Bible study group. In reality, faith settings are a natural target for abusers because there are a large number of children, a shortage of people willing to volunteer or lead, and a culture of trust that assumes that no person with a religious commitment would abuse children. The widespread number of abuse cases in the Catholic church is the consequence of this stereotype. Another setting that is wrongfully believed to be immune from abuse is the home.

- Any type of childhood sexual abuse has serious consequences in childhood and adulthood, and it is not forgotten by the child.
- It is wrong to believe that childhood sexual abuse, especially if it is not rape, is "not that bad."

People assume that children will forget the experience of being sexually abused. People also assume that addressing the abuse will create worse consequences than simply ignoring it. But there is overwhelming evidence that unaddressed childhood sexual abuse creates immediate and long-term difficulties for children and adults.

Let us pause and think about the wrongful beliefs that are corrected above. It is possible, and even likely, that one or more of them prevented people from recognizing abuse when it happened to you. Maybe you believed some of these wrongful beliefs yourself, such as might be the case if you tell yourself, "It wasn't that bad, really; he didn't rape me, he just fondled me." Thinking about these beliefs now might signal this as a time to journal your reactions. As outlined in the Introduction, using a journal as you read this book provides a means for reflection. You might write out what wrongful beliefs you have held, or others in your life have held, and your reactions to them. You can also write out what action steps you can take, now or later, to correct these beliefs. The Resources section at the end of the chapter contains material to help you in this goal; see the entry for the National Sexual Violence Resource Center and for the book by Courtois (2014).

HOW DOES CHILDHOOD SEXUAL ABUSE INTERFERE WITH DEVELOPMENT?

We can think of the damaging effects of childhood sexual abuse as happening in two different ways. The first is that childhood sexual abuse prevents or interferes with "normal"—that is, typical or customary—child development. The second is that childhood sexual abuse causes additional damages in childhood. This section of the chapter describes how childhood sexual abuse interferes with normal development in children and adolescents. The next section discusses specific types of damage that occur after childhood sexual abuse.

Milestones in Normal Child Development

What is normal child development? If you are around a child as he or she grows from an infant to a toddler to a child, you witness a range of amazing changes. *Development* refers to the tasks the growing child has to accomplish, just like development as a talented musician means many hours of practice. There are physical tasks to be learned: sitting up, walking, kicking a ball. There are also socioemotional tasks: talking to others, taking turns. Child development professionals speak of these tasks as "milestones" because most children do these things by a certain age. Caregivers are concerned that a child is having problems in development if the child does not meet the milestones.

There are parallel developmental tasks that are psychological and occur in stages. Erik Erikson (1968) described tasks that begin in infancy and last through later life; the following tasks are applicable to children from birth to age 18:

- *Stage 1: Trust versus mistrust.* During the first year of life, the infant must develop a relationship with caregivers and with the world in general. Is the world a safe place or not? If care-givers provide consistent and reliable care, the infant develops trust. But if care is harsh or inconsistent or not predictable, the infant develops mistrust. Most importantly, that mistrust carries over to other interpersonal relationships.

- *Stage 2: Autonomy versus shame and doubt.* After the first year and until about age 3, the child becomes more active. If the caregiver encourages the child to explore within safe limits, the child develops autonomy. With autonomy, the child becomes confident and secure in his or her own ability. How-ever, if children are overly criticized or controlled, they feel inadequate (shame) or worry about their abilities (doubt).
- *Stage 3: Initiative versus guilt.* Between ages 3 and 5, children's lives center on play and interaction with other children. When children challenge themselves, such as by being determined to go down the slide, and succeed, they develop initiative. They also learn to regulate their emotions, getting support from other children or from caregivers to deal with negative emo-tions such as disappointment or anger. But when children are prevented from trying at all or are punished for failure, they develop guilt that interferes with trying again.
- *Stage 4: Industry versus inferiority.* Between the ages of 5 and 12, children are increasingly independent in their lives. Teachers and other children play different roles than parents and become a source of self-esteem. When children are encouraged to develop specific competencies (such as playing a musical instrument, learning a sport, writing poetry, being in a play), they feel competent, have a sense of pride, and are industrious. If they fail, or do not try, or see their teachers and peers as being too demanding and critical, then a sense of inferiority occurs.
- *Stage 5: Identity versus role confusion.* During adolescence, children are becoming adults. They are searching for their

personal values, beliefs, and goals. They are seeing their future in terms of a career, intimate relationships, family structure, and so on. There are challenges in this process, some physical, as in puberty, and some psychosocial, as in friendships and relationships. Learning to commit to others and having integrity in the self leads to a solid identity, whereas being prevented from exploration or forced into conformity leads to confusion.

Childhood Development When a Child Is Sexually Abused

Knowing the tasks involved in each stage of development allows us to understand how childhood sexual abuse interferes with development. There are three types of interference—shame, profound fear, and damaged relationships.

SHAME

The first interference is the deep sense of shame. Children who are abused cannot understand why the abuse is happening to them. It is impossible for the child to conclude that the adult perpetrator, most likely a family member or trusted adult, is bad. Therefore, the child concludes that he or she is bad and deserving of the abusive treatment. Often, a child responds to abuse with behaviors that themselves bring condemnation, such as acting out, withdrawing, running away, and the like. Receiving disapproval for these normal responses to abuse leads to more shame and to self-loathing.

It is important to differentiate between healthy and unhealthy shame. If I commit an action that harmed another person, and I know that I did wrong, I should feel shame. Shame stimulates us to change our behaviors in the future. But unhealthy shame is not attached to an action but to the self. It is the belief that the self is and always will be wrong.

Profound Fear

The second interference is the development of profound fear. It is normal for fear to follow an experience of harm. As humans, we learn not to get ourselves again into a situation that caused us fear and harm. But when the abuse cannot be avoided and is perpetrated by a supposedly trusted person, the fear cannot be escaped. That fear is shown in several ways. One way is through self-protective behaviors such as running away or hiding. A second way is through compulsive behaviors, such as hair pulling or skin picking or thumb sucking well beyond the normal age. A third way is through physical health symptoms, such as nausea or headaches, that show that fear is being converted to physical disorders.

If the fear is too much, children respond with emotional numbness. "Alexithymia" is the word for when someone does not experience emotions or has difficulty distinguishing feelings from bodily sensations. An extreme form of numbing is "dissociation," which is the word for the experience in which a person detaches from reality. When a person is dissociating, they may not experience the passage of time, or they may be physically present but not feel that they are in their own body.

Damaged Relationships

The third interference in normal development is related to the fact that childhood sexual abuse mostly occurs in relationships. When the abuse occurs in the context of a primary child–adult relationship, the child fails to learn how to be in a relationship with a parent or with a family member or with any adult. Some abused children who are not valued for who they are turn to attempts to be valued for what they do by becoming "superstar" children; these children work hard at finding out what the adults in their lives value, and then they perform those desirable actions. They often appear mature because they want validation from adults. Other abused children give up on pleasing others and become completely focused on meeting their own unmet basic needs. When an individual is completely focused on the self, the ability to sense and understand the feelings of others, called "empathy," is undeveloped. Without empathy, mutual interpersonal relationships cannot occur.

To summarize, normal development is blocked by several aspects of childhood sexual abuse. First, the shame that victims of sexual abuse experience in interpersonal relationships prevents them from gaining full autonomy, initiative, industry, and identity. Second, the presence of overwhelming emotional distress and anxiety leads victims to focus on coming up with coping strategies to deal with those emotions rather than dealing with necessary tasks in normal life. Third, relationships in which children should learn life lessons become warped by abuse and cannot serve this purpose. Overall, trust is damaged, which undermines all the developmental tasks.

HOW DOES CHILDHOOD SEXUAL ABUSE DAMAGE THE CHILD'S BODY, MIND, AND EMOTIONS?

One of the worst stereotypes about childhood sexual abuse is that it is "no big deal" and most likely to be forgotten by the child without lingering effects. In reality, survivors experience long-term trauma. In her classic book on trauma, psychiatrist Judith Herman (1997) drafted a definition of *trauma* that remains accurate today:

> Psychological trauma is an affliction of the powerless. At the moment of trauma, the victim is rendered helpless by overwhelming force. When the force is that of nature, we speak of disasters. When the force is that of other human beings, we speak of atrocities. Traumatic events overwhelm the ordinary systems of care that give people a sense of control, connection, and meaning. (p. 33)

This definition applies even more when the victim is a child. A child is dependent on adults for care and cannot protect himself or herself. Additionally, children are developmentally different from adults, and their systems of "control, connection, and meaning" are not yet in place. This section of the chapter discusses damage to various aspects of the child's physical and psychosocial well-being.

Why is it important for you to have this information? A reader of an early draft of this book thought that covering the many damages of childhood sexual abuse was "too dark." I remind you that I also am a survivor, of incest. Before I received treatment, I truly believed that things I suffered from were my fault and somehow uniquely me. It was only as I learned more about childhood sexual abuse from my therapist, and began to read relevant books, that I learned that everything I experienced was "typical" for an adult survivor of childhood sexual abuse. Christine Courtois (2014), a pioneer in the study of incest, wrote a book on the topic called *It's Not You, It's What Happened to You*. And that title is exactly right. These damages happened to you; they are not who you are. And they are not too dark to the people who experience them. They are simply the reality.

Before moving on, I want to state three cautions. First, the damages I discuss below have been the experience of survivors of childhood sexual abuse. But rarely does a single child experience all of them. Second, as I describe in Chapter 4, some children have resilience resources that "buffer," or protect, them from some of the problems that can occur later in life. Third, you may find that reading about these problems helps you understand your life. However, you may find that this section of the chapter is triggering, in which case you should skip it and return to it later when you are ready. Recall the experience of triggering discussed in the Introduction; when you are triggered, your emotional reactions to something you read, see, or hear are very intense because it arouses memories associated with trauma.

The aftereffects of childhood sexual abuse have been documented in specific "domains"—that is, areas of human functioning—that are briefly described below. The Resources section at the end of this chapter lists books and websites that provide more information on damage that results from childhood sexual abuse.

Emotional Stress and Stress Reduction Behaviors

Child victims of sexual abuse experience specific stress-related problems, especially because the trauma of abuse usually happens over a period of time and cannot be escaped. Thus, the child is in a steady state of fear and anticipation, which creates more stress and therefore more stress reduction behaviors. The emotions that signal stress are anxiety, fear, confusion, depression, anger, shame, and guilt. Stress reduction methods are more limited for younger children, who do not have the independence of older adolescents or adults, and therefore young children focus on avoidance behaviors such as numbing, hiding, dissociating, and "becoming invisible."

Self-Perception

Abused children do not have the capacity to believe they are good and deserving of love when they are in a situation of betrayal and entrapment. They may try to act "good" if they believe that being that way would stop the abuse. But thinking they are alone in this situation creates shame and feelings of unworthiness. Developmental psychologists believe that children develop pictures of how they relate to the outside world called "internal working models." For children who receive regular, loving responses from their caregivers, their working models see themselves as worthy of love and their caregivers as trustworthy. But when children are abused, their working models are damaged. They see themselves as unworthy of love, and they see their caregivers as untrustworthy.

Problems in Learning, Including Educational Problems

Researchers have documented that high levels of distress—fear, anxiety, vigilance—experienced by abused children interfere with cognitive development and the ability to learn. Their brains are literally focused only on survival, which reduces the brain's ability to form the new connections required for learning. Some abused children develop memory problems, learning problems, an inability to concentrate, and other problems that interfere in their education. An additional problem is that childhood sexual abuse is associated with school avoidance. Children may refuse to go to school outright, or they may create reasons why they should not go, which usually consist of vague symptoms such as headaches, stomachaches, nausea, or dizziness.

Physical Problems

Abused children often develop medical symptoms that are difficult to diagnose. Some of these are directly associated with the abuse, such as headaches and stomachaches, bedwetting, and urinary tract infections. Other problems come about from high levels of stress. Researchers have documented that abuse "dysregulates," or creates an abnormality in, the system that controls the stress response (i.e., the hypothalamus in the brain, the pituitary gland in the body, and the adrenal cortex in the kidney). When normal systems for stress control do not develop as they should, the child may experience low appetite, nausea, dizziness, fatigue, and vomiting.

Sexual Effects

Sometimes abuse results in an awareness of sexual behaviors that is age inappropriate. In other words, these children may be aware of and show sexual behaviors not typical for children. Examples are exhibitionism and simulating sexual acts with children or toys.

However, other children display the complete opposite, avoiding any physical contact. These children may startle when touched, feel disgusted by their bodies, or engage in self-mutilation.

Interpersonal Relationships

The abused child has damaged trust in caregivers, adults, and other persons. Therefore, their relationships are characterized by lack of trust. They may be excessively needy for emotional attachment. They may also be unusually avoidant, appearing uninterested in any type of interpersonal relationship. Their internal working model creates difficulties in emotional attachment to other persons, including other children as well as adults.

In summary, the degree and range of life functions affected by childhood sexual abuse is extensive. By no means can we conclude in the face of all available evidence that childhood sexual abuse, even a single event, is "no big deal." It is a deeply damaging abuse of trust that echoes throughout childhood and into adulthood.

HOW DOES CHILDHOOD SEXUAL ABUSE DAMAGE THE ADULT'S EMOTIONS, MIND, AND BODY?

The difficulties of childhood abuse do not go away with time, although they come to take a different shape. Difficulties continue in emotions and in relationships; new problems come about in physical health and in memory.

Emotional Distress

The difficult emotions associated with abuse during childhood continue into adulthood. Anxiety and fear remain and may be increased by transitions and traumas that occur in the life of the adult. The adult may experience symptoms such as panic attacks, circumscribed

27

fears such as fear of the dark or of being alone, and various phobias. Depression is likely to be persistent, manifested by long-term feelings of sadness, detachment, and grief. These emotional difficulties may prompt the adult to use coping responses that numb or deaden the feelings, such as substance use and abuse and addictive behaviors such as gambling, that create more problems.

Childhood sexual abuse may result in symptoms in adults that are diagnosed as posttraumatic stress disorder (PTSD). PTSD consists of clusters of symptoms that follow a traumatic event (American Psychiatric Association, 2013). The first cluster is *reexperiencing*. Reexperiencing includes unwanted and uncontrollable memories of the trauma, dreams in which the content is related to the trauma, and flashbacks during which the person feels or acts as if the trauma were actually happening in the present. The second cluster is *persistent avoidance* of any reminder of the event, including locations, people, objects, and the like. The third cluster is *negative cognitions* (thoughts) *and mood* (feelings) associated with the trauma, such as an inability to remember the event, negative beliefs about the world such as "no one can be trusted," and an inability to experience positive emotions. The fourth cluster is *arousal*, which includes hypervigilance, problems with concentration, and sleep disturbance.

In summary, adults who were sexually abused as children have difficulty recognizing their feelings, expressing their feelings, and calming themselves when they experience distress. Depression, anxiety, shame, confusion, and fear are common. The constant arousal they experienced as a child created changes in their brains and in the way they experience feelings.

Pathways to Revictimization

The term *revictimization* refers to the repeated occurrence of "interpersonal victimization," or adverse events caused by other persons.

These events can be sexual, such as date rape; violent, such as intimate partner violence; or interpersonal, such as being stalked. Data reveal that people who were sexually abused during childhood are 2 to 3 times more likely to experience revictimization as adults (Widom et al., 2008). Revictimization creates additional trauma in the life of the adult who was abused as a child, and therefore significantly more difficulties. Researchers have attempted to define "pathways" to revictimization because preventing revictimization is an important goal. But a firm understanding of those pathways still is not available. It is likely that the exploitation involved in childhood sexual abuse resulted in an inability to define boundaries for the self, and thus the adult is less likely to recognize or remove themselves from dangerous situations.

Perceptions of the Self

A consistent finding from research is that adults who were sexually abused as children have negative views of the self. These adults often see themselves as unlovable, dirty, worthless, different from others, and "bad." Because child victims cannot understand the reasons the abuse occurred, blaming themselves leads them to believe that something they did led to the abuse, and this belief often lasts into adulthood. Many adult victims do not understand that their problems and symptoms are universal among abuse victims, leading to the belief that they are alone in the world. Even small symptoms, such as food aversions or a preoccupation with violence, may lead adult victims to believe they are "crazy."

These perceptions of the self are reinforced by life difficulties that all adults experience. When transitions or traumas create uncertainty, adult victims do not have the necessary self-confidence to push through the trauma or transition. They experience hopelessness and despair, concluding that the world will never change for them and that their lives will be marked only by failure. Whether the difficulty is in their occupation, or interpersonal relationships, or family life, these adults assume that the reason for the difficulty is a completely personal failure.

Physical Effects

Abuse has many lasting physical effects. The physical body "keeps the score," in the words of Bessel van der Kolk (2014), who wrote of the experiences of the body after abuse. Adults with a history of childhood sexual abuse have more problems than adults without such a history in many health categories. Their general health is poorer. They report more gastrointestinal diseases such as irritable bowel syndrome. They have more gynecological symptoms, such as chronic pelvic pain. They have more pain-related diseases such as back pain and jaw (temporomandibular joint) pain. More of them report cardiopulmonary problems such as irregular heartbeat and shortness of breath. Lastly, obesity rates are higher among adults with a history of childhood sexual abuse. Insights From Psychology 1.1 presents a research investigation comparing the physical, mental, and behavioral health of adults who were and were not abused as children.

Sexual Effects

Childhood sexual abuse creates a disturbance in normal sexual development. Previously abused adolescents may be more sexually experienced than peers or may regard certain sexualized interactions as normal. Survivor adults may have unusually frequent sexual activity. This pattern of behavior leads to high-risk sexual practices, such as sex with strangers or unprotected sex. Survivor adults may also completely avoid sexual contact.

Insights From Psychology 1.1

What Do We Know About the Connection Between Adult Health Problems and Childhood Sexual Abuse?

The long-term effects of childhood sexual abuse are becoming recognized as a significant public health problem. Many physical health problems, such as generalized pain, gastrointestinal problems, obesity, chronic fatigue, and allergies, are overrepresented among adults who were abused as children. Understanding the adult health implications of childhood sexual abuse is important in ensuring that survivors can obtain the best possible care.

A 2020 study of health among four groups of women investigated whether childhood sexual abuse predicted poor health as adults (Rosen et al., 2020). More than 500 participants completed a set of questionnaires about childhood abuse, their overall health, disability from pain and other chronic conditions, and concerns about illness, as well as a measure of attachment. The participants' ages ranged from 18 to 46 years, and they were primarily White (67%), with Asian (16%) and Biracial (12%) the next most frequent self-descriptors.

The results revealed two important findings. First, all of the health measures showed that childhood sexual abuse predicted poorer adult health compared with nonabused participants. Survivors had worse general health, their health problems interfered with normal life to a greater extent, and they engaged in fewer health-seeking behaviors such as doctor visits. Second, the survivors had attachment difficulties and were less secure in their relationships, and this insecurity also predicted increased health problems. The authors suggested that adult survivors who do not trust others or are unable to establish solid friendships may experience health problems because of a lack of social connection, in addition to the problems directly caused by abuse in childhood.

There are also difficulties in sexual functioning. Survivors may find it difficult to become sexually aroused or perform sexually. Female survivors may have difficulties with lubrication or reaching orgasm. Male survivors may experience problems obtaining or maintaining an erection. Many survivors experience pain during intercourse, sometimes because of physical injury from the abuse. Overall, sexual contact may raise feelings of disgust, or fear, or guilt that interfere with sexual enjoyment.

In summary, experiencing sexual abuse affects virtually all of the components of normal adult sexual activity. For survivors, physiological effects of the abuse may affect sexual behaviors, intimacy may be frightening, specific sexual acts may feel like a boundary intrusion, and flashbacks of the abuse may occur during sex.

Memory and Traumatic Events

One of the most misunderstood aspects of childhood sexual abuse is its effect on memory. Many people understand memory as a collection of videos taken over time that were accurately recorded and can be replayed on demand. Others think of memory as a collection of digital files that can be opened or stored, again to be accessed on demand. Still others believe that memory is a walk through the woods, where there are paths that are well traveled and paths not so well traveled, and that walking toward the less traveled paths will make them reappear and be familiar again. For some, memory is a dark room where they must search for the past with a flashlight.

Each of these metaphors falls short of describing the amazing complexity of memory. Memory resides in several areas of our brain, each holding a different function; for example, the memory-retrieving function sits in the hippocampus. When we want to recover a memory, it must be reconstructed from elements scattered throughout our brain. When we "forget" a memory, we are temporarily or permanently unable to retrieve the information or construct the memory.

This topic is complex. But to summarize, here is what psychologists now believe about memory:

- Not every aspect of an event is maintained in memory. One of the most important influences on what is maintained is the presence of positive versus negative emotions. Negative emotions such as fear and confusion make it more difficult to accurately store the event in memory.
- The process by which a memory is retrieved has an influence on what is retrieved. For example, being asked questions about an event prompts different types of memory than does viewing pictures of the event.
- The completeness of a memory and the accuracy of a memory are separate. Some memories are recalled inaccurately, and others are accurate but only partially recalled.

An important understanding of memory is that memories of trauma are completely different from memories of normal events (see Staniloiu et al., 2020). The traumatic experience is difficult to incorporate into memory because it occurs in the context of extreme emotion, confusion, and disruption. That context means that the memory essentially exists apart from memories of normal events, and the memory therefore is difficult to access. Adults who were sexually abused as children frequently retain little or no memory of the trauma, and when those memories are recovered, they initially appear in a fragmented, incomplete, and vague way. Over time, a more organized form of the memory may appear.

An additional aspect of this topic is that sexually abused children do not have fully developed brains. Therefore, the way in which trauma is encoded (that is, processed and stored) for them is affected both by the trauma itself and by their brain's lack of maturity. The accuracy of adult survivors' reports of abuse is sometimes criticized because their memories of the abuse are incomplete or they have no memories at all. But it is a significant misunderstanding of trauma memories to assume that because the memories are incomplete or absent, the trauma did not happen.

Other Effects

Survivors of childhood sexual abuse face many other issues in adult life, and it is impossible to describe them all. Parenting, relationships within the biological family, drug and alcohol use disorders, addictions, eating disorders, and intimacy may be affected. In addition, the ways in which children learned to cope, such as numbing, avoidance, dissociation, denial, minimizing, and forgetting, create issues in adulthood. Some survivors seek to maintain control at all costs, or create chaos, or find safety within rigid boundaries offered by religion or a controlling partner, or engage in self-destructive behavior; these strategies are not effective for living a healthy life. Psychologists speak of such strategies as the "compounding effects" of childhood abuse, which means that how survivors cope with the abuse becomes ingrained in their way of interacting with the world, and those coping methods then create new problems as survivors grow older.

FINDING A NEW PATH FORWARD: FROM ME TO YOU

You are likely to be feeling quite overwhelmed by this chapter. It is so difficult to read about all the adult problems that are a result of childhood abuse, and it may seem to you that a life free of those problems is impossible. The theme of this book is that you can improve your life by focusing on processes that increase your resilience and your ability to change. But it is also true that if you are being controlled by problems like those described in this chapter, you should consider seeking professional help. That topic is covered in more detail in Chapter 3.

I am now in my late 60s, and I have had a life marked by the abuse I experienced as a child. It was not until I was an adult that I began to find a new path. I did get counseling, on more than one occasion. And that helped me greatly. But even with that, I was left with things I did not want as part of my life anymore. I self-soothed with eating, and I was overweight. I was fearful of being alone, and before I could go to bed I would check all the doors many times to be sure they were locked. And so on. But there came a time when I decided to use new coping strategies that were healthier. And one by one, those old patterns began to go away.

You can change. When you were a child, you had few options for coping with your abuse. You did what you had to do, literally, to survive. Now, as an adult, you have more options. You can change patterns of behavior that are destructive. You can build a healthier self. You are unique in your history and your current abilities and resources, but you also share in the experiences of many people. Knowing that you are not alone may be a comfort to you, as I hope it will. You have no reason to be ashamed, and you have every reason to know that you did the best you could under horrific circumstances. You are a survivor, rather than a victim, when you begin to see a new path forward.

RESOURCES

Digital Resources

- The Joyful Heart Foundation (https://www.joyfulheart foundation.org) was founded in 2004 with a focus on sexual assault, domestic violence, and child abuse. The foundation provides education and advocacy resources for adult survivors.

- The National Sexual Violence Resource Center (https://www. nsvrc.org) was established to provide leadership in responding to the needs of survivors of violence. The center provides a list of resources for childhood sexual abuse survivors (https:// www.nsvrc.org/sites/default/files/2014-09/nsvrc_publications_ resource-list_online-resources-for-survivors.pdf).
- The Survivors Network of those Abused by Priests (SNAP; https://www.snapnetwork.org) is the largest and oldest organization for survivors of abuse by clergy or institutional authorities associated with churches. SNAP has local affiliations with support groups as well as a large collection of helpful resources available through the website.

Crisis Hotlines

- Stop It Now (1-888-PREVENT [773-8368]; https://stopitnow. org) was founded in 1992 to prevent sexual abuse of children. This organization offers online resources and training for parents and caregivers intended to prevent childhood sexual abuse.
- The Rape, Abuse, and Incest National Network, known as RAINN (1-800-656-HOPE [4673]; https://www.rainn.org), offers resources including information on laws and policies. The network partners with more than 1,000 local sexual assault service providers.

Print Resources

- *Beyond Surviving: The Final State in Recovery From Sexual Abuse*, by Rachel Grant (iUniverse Books, 2012). This workbook covers abuse-related topics such as challenging false beliefs and rewiring the brain. Each segment is short (two or three pages) and has information and exercises.

- *Healing the Trauma of Abuse: A Women's Workbook*, by Mary Ellen Copeland and Maxine Harris (New Harbinger Publications, 2000). This workbook is a step-by-step guide to recovery for women after sexual, emotional, or physical abuse in childhood or adulthood. It covers topics under the general categories of empowerment, trauma recovery, and life changes.

- *It's Not You, It's What Happened to You: Complex Trauma and Treatment*, by Christine Courtois (Elements Behavioral Health, 2014). This book is so important that I have included it in several chapters' Resources section. The author is a psychologist who specializes in the treatment of trauma, particularly the aftereffects of childhood sexual abuse. Manifestations of childhood trauma in the life of the adult are presented in a clear and thoughtful manner.

CHAPTER 2

UNDERSTANDING COMPLEX TRAUMA

Recovery Milestones

This chapter will help you

1. **learn** accurate information about trauma and
2. **discover** the concept of complex trauma and **understand** why it is a better explanation for the experience of, and damage caused by, childhood sexual abuse.

Trauma is a ubiquitous word: It is used virtually all the time for an unlimited range of events and situations. People describe everyday events such as a bad haircut or a social mistake as a trauma. You read in social media about trauma, vicarious trauma, or trauma response training. It is a good thing that society is alert to the presence and effects of trauma. Unfortunately, some information spread on social media contains misunderstandings or stereotypes. It is important for you to understand facts about trauma that are based in the science of psychology. My first goal for this chapter is to provide that firm foundation for you.

Even more important is learning what type of trauma best characterizes your situation. As we will see, there are a variety of ways to understand trauma, and the more straightforward ways may not best describe the aftereffects of childhood sexual abuse. Psychologists have developed a new picture of certain kinds of trauma such as childhood sexual abuse. That new picture is called "complex trauma." The second goal for this chapter is for you to learn about characteristics and consequences of complex trauma.

WHAT IS TRAUMA?

Historically, "trauma" referred to physical injuries, occurring in and on the body, with the potential for causing death or prolonged disability. Thus, an emergency room physician might describe a patient after an automobile accident as having "extensive trauma." That label means that the patient has severe injuries—for example, burns, broken bones, and lacerations, as well as changes in blood pressure because of extensive bleeding. In the context of combat, "trauma" is used to describe severe injuries to soldiers, such as those resulting from the explosion of a roadside improvised explosive device ("IED"). The physical damage from that type of trauma often includes injury to the brain. "Trauma" is also used for psychosocial problems that result from certain types of events called "traumatic stressors"; this term reflects the understanding that these events are "traumatic" for the people experiencing them and "stressors" because of the cause–effect relationship between the event and its aftereffects.

The *Diagnostic and Statistical Manual of Mental Disorders* (fifth ed.; American Psychiatric Association, 2013), which lists agreed-upon categories of psychosocial difficulties, explains the types of events necessary for a diagnosis of posttraumatic stress disorder (PTSD) to be made. Those events include exposure to actual or threatened death, serious injury, or sexual violence by directly experiencing the event, witnessing the event as it occurred to others, learning that the event occurred to a family member or close friend, or being exposed repeatedly to details of such events (such as with first responders). There are many events that meet this definition, including environmental disasters, such as a tornado, hurricane, or wildfire, and human-made disasters, such as an explosion at a factory, an automobile or bus or train accident, or a mass shooting.

However, people can also experience trauma after experiences that may not appear to be traumatic to observers. Ronnie Janoff-Bulman (1989), a psychologist, drew on 15 years of research with survivors of overwhelming life events when she characterized *trauma* as an event that shatters our assumptions and beliefs about the world. Those assumptions tend to fall into three categories. The first category includes assumptions that the world is a benevolent place; examples of beliefs in this category are "people are essentially kind" and "misfortune occurs rarely." The second category includes assumptions that life is meaningful and not random; examples of beliefs in this category are "people get what they deserve" and "good things happen to good people." The third category includes assumptions that are self-affirming; examples are "I am worthwhile" and "I am a decent person and deserve good outcomes in life." When an event or experience shatters a person's basic assumptions about the world, he or she is a victim of trauma, whether or not the event is perceived by others as traumatic.

To summarize, here is what we know about trauma:

- Traumas are events that cause or threaten death or disability to the person experiencing it or to a family member or close friend who learns of it.
- Traumas also are events that shatter our assumptions about the world: An example of such an assumption is that there is

justice in the world and therefore bad things do not happen to good people such as ourselves.

IS TRAUMA THE BEST WAY TO UNDERSTAND CHILDHOOD SEXUAL ABUSE?

The mechanisms of trauma are danger and fear. Danger is an important stimulus for humans; a "stimulus" is something that causes a response. For humans in prehistoric times, seeing a large predator (a dangerous stimulus) was linked to fear and then escape. Even for us today, danger is linked to fear and escape. We use the term "fight or flight" to indicate that our usual response to a dangerous stimulus is to either act against it or run away.

Fear rouses emotional systems. For example, fear energizes both the fight response and the flight response. Fear prompts a seeking system in the brain, which searches for goal-directed behaviors, such as escape, and assists learning by associating certain cues with the dangerous situation. Fear is also linked to panic, which moves the individual toward others in the environment for help with the situation. But when the dangerous stimulus is no longer present, fear also is no longer present. Once the predator was gone, the fear went away. In our lives, once the dangerous event that gives us fear passes, our fear also passes.

How well does this set of mechanisms—danger and fear—fit with victims' experiences of abuse? Children who are sexually abused are in danger and deeply frightened. But they cannot escape from the abuse, as they could from a predator in the wild, because they are trapped in the relationship in which the abuse occurs or cannot avoid the perpetrator. Another difference between trauma and childhood sexual abuse is that after trauma, most people recover their pretrauma lives. But after childhood sexual abuse, the consequences continue, even long after the abuse ends. A better term for the trauma of childhood sexual abuse is "complex trauma."

WHAT IS COMPLEX TRAUMA?

Complex trauma is defined as the experience of multiple, chronic, and prolonged, developmentally adverse traumatic events, most often of an interpersonal nature, and often within the child's caregiving system (Spinazzola et al., 2018). Psychologists who study childhood sexual abuse see the concept of complex trauma as a better way of understanding the experience of the child. You experienced complex trauma because of the childhood sexual abuse you suffered. So it is important that you understand what this type of trauma involves.

Multiple Traumatic Events

Most traumas in the lives of adults are single events—for example, a car accident or a disaster such as a hurricane. People who experience multiple events in challenging circumstances, such as victims of childhood sexual abuse, suffer the extreme results of repeated trauma. In repeated traumatic events, the victim is unable to escape from or exercise control over the trauma. So the frequency of the events, as well as the individual's loss of control, overwhelm the victim's well-being.

Chronic and Prolonged

Childhood sexual abuse can vary in its frequency (how many times it happens) and duration (how long it lasts). But most often, childhood sexual abuse is an ongoing series of events that escalate in intensity. That escalation occurs as the perpetrator increases the type of sexual activity with the child, for example, from watching, to fondling, to penetration and forced sexual acts. Even if the child discloses the abuse, it does not always stop, especially if the child is not believed (see Pipe et al., 2007).

43

Developmentally Adverse

Chapter 1 described the developmental interference caused by childhood sexual abuse. If you did not read that section of the chapter yet, the following is a brief summary: Childhood involves mastering a series of psychosocial and physical developmental tasks ("milestones"). A physical developmental task is learning to walk. Psychosocial developmental tasks include learning to trust a caregiver, learning give-and-take in a relationship with another person, and learning to deal with adversity and failure. When caregivers consistently attend to children's needs, children successfully learn to deal with themselves and their environment. When caregivers mistreat children, children become disordered in their sense of themselves and their understanding of the world.

Of an Interpersonal Nature

As noted in Chapter 1, 90% of childhood sexual abuse happens in a relationship: an ongoing series of contacts between a child and someone the child knows and trusts or is dependent on, or who is an unavoidable part of the child's environment. The damages from the interpersonal nature of the abuse are in attachment, trust, and social learning. The child is "prewired" to learn many things in relationships with people. Childhood sexual abuse disrupts that capacity for learning by shattering trust in the relationship but forcing a continual dependence on it or eliminating the possibility of escape.

Within the Child's Caregiving System

It is developmentally impossible for the child to blame the parent or other caregiver for the abuse. Therefore, the child blames himself or herself. For the blame to make sense, the child concludes that the abuse and rejection are deserved. That complete reversal of the normal caregiving system is what creates "unhealthy shame," or the belief that the self is and always will be wrong.

Childhood Sexual Abuse as a Betrayal

The interpersonal violation involved in childhood sexual abuse perpetrated by an individual whom the child cares for, is dependent on, or trusts is processed in the child's brain and remembered differently than violations perpetrated by an individual with whom the victim does not have such a connection. Essentially, the abuse is a betrayal of the existing interpersonal connection between victim and perpetrator. A trauma that involves interpersonal betrayal is termed a "betrayal trauma" (Freyd & Birrell, 2013). Betrayal traumas happen between parent and child, teacher and child, faith leader and child, camp counselor and child, coach and child, doctor and child, or the child and any individual in an ongoing relationship with the child.

Because the child cannot escape or believes it necessary to remain in the abusive relationship, the child develops "blindness" to the betrayal and does not identify the abuse as such. Betrayal blindness allows the child to maintain an attachment to the caregiver despite the abuse. It serves as a mechanism for survival during childhood. But in adulthood, that blindness causes the survivor to be unable to remember the abuse, to remember it as nonthreatening ("it wasn't that big a deal"), to normalize the abuse ("that is just how he was"), or to blame the self ("it was my fault").

Other Types of Complex Trauma

Complex trauma includes a range of experiences. Ford (2017) characterized complex trauma as intentional interpersonal acts that are inescapable and cause injury that is potentially irreparable. Other experiences conform to this characterization, among them human

45

trafficking, war, torture, genocide, and other forms of captivity or slavery. Although complex trauma often begins in childhood, it can also continue or begin in adulthood. All complex trauma experiences include psychological or physical oppression and subjugation.

To summarize, complex trauma in victims of childhood sexual abuse is different from other types of trauma in the following ways:

- The trauma happens repeatedly over a lengthy period of time.
- It often begins in childhood, when mature adult systems of thinking and feeling are not yet in place.
- The trauma is inflicted on the child by an adult within an interpersonal connection.
- The adult perpetrating the abuse is likely someone the child trusts, cares for, and depends on.

WHAT ARE ADVERSE CHILDHOOD EXPERIENCES?

You may have heard about adverse childhood experiences ("ACEs") and wondered whether those experiences include childhood sexual abuse. This label is used for experiences that happen during childhood (age 0 to 17 years) that are potentially traumatic. Self-Assessment 2.1 provides an ACE questionnaire. Public health efforts focused on ACEs grew out of original research in California that demonstrated that multiple adverse events in childhood lead to poor health among adults (Felitti et al., 1998). For example, adults with four or more ACE events had a significantly higher risk of heart disease, cancer, lung disease, and liver disease. This study and other research on the topic led medical professionals to recognize that diseases occur in adults for reasons that may have had their beginnings in childhood. This insight has led in turn to increased awareness in education, criminal justice, medicine, and other systems of interpersonal care of the ACE history of their users.

Self-Assessment 2.1

What Is Your ACE Score?

Directions: Read the questions, and write either a "yes" or a "no" in your journal or note-taking app.

Before your 18th birthday,

1. Did a parent or other adult in the household often or very often swear at you, insult you, put you down, or humiliate you? *or* act in a way that made you afraid that you might be physically hurt?
2. Did a parent or other adult in the household often or very often push, grab, slap, or throw something at you? *or* ever hit you so hard that you had marks or were injured?
3. Did an adult or a person at least 5 years older than you ever touch or fondle you or have you touch their body in a sexual way? *or* attempt or actually have oral, anal, or vaginal intercourse with you?
4. Did you often or very often feel that no one in your family loved you or thought you were important or special? *or* your family didn't look out for each other, feel close to each other, or support each other?
5. Did you often or very often feel that you didn't have enough to eat, had to wear dirty clothes, and had no one to protect you? *or* your parents were too drunk or high to take care of you or take you to the doctor if you needed it?
6. Was a biological parent ever lost to you through divorce, abandonment, or other reason?
7. Was your mother or stepmother often or very often pushed, grabbed, slapped, or had something thrown at her? *or* sometimes, often, or very often kicked, bitten, hit with a fist, or hit with something hard? *or* ever repeatedly hit over at least a few minutes or threatened with a gun or a knife?
8. Did you live with someone who was a problem drinker or alcoholic, or who used street drugs?
9. Was a household member depressed or mentally ill, or did a household member attempt suicide?
10. Did a household member go to prison?

(continues)

Self-Assessment 2.1 (*Continued*)

Add up your "yes" answers; you'll have a number from 0 to 10. That is your ACE score.

What does your ACE score mean? ACE scores are not a crystal ball, and you will not automatically have poorer health as an adult if you have a high ACE score. But the risk of having serious health problems has been shown to increase as the ACE score increases, especially for people with a score of 4 or higher.

Note. From *The ACE Test: Adverse Childhood Experiences*, by Stop Abuse Campaign, n.d. (https://stopabusecampaign.org/what-are-adverse-childhood-experiences/take-your-ace-test/). Copyright 2021 by Stop Abuse Campaign. Reprinted with permission.

ACEs are common across the population. More than two thirds of adults have one ACE, and 25% have three or more (Centers for Disease Control and Prevention, 2020). ACE scores explain population-wide patterns of health risk for adults from adverse events in childhood. But the questionnaire does not include some childhood experiences that we know are associated with later problems in adulthood, such as bullying, death of a parent or caregiver, or community violence. In addition, you can have a low ACE score even though you experienced childhood sexual abuse. ACE scores are widespread now for helping measure childhood difficulties; many versions of the ACE measure have been developed and circulated. The concept of childhood adversity is important, but the ACE measure itself does not reflect the range of components of complex trauma or the enormity of the damage from childhood sexual abuse.

WHAT ARE THE CONSEQUENCES OF COMPLEX TRAUMA?

Just as complex trauma is a different experience from trauma, the consequences of complex trauma are also different. Let us start with a review of the consequences of trauma. PTSD is the term for symptoms that are aftereffects of trauma. Recall from Chapter 1 that there are four clusters of symptoms: unwanted and uncontrollable reexperiencing of the trauma, avoidance of any reminders of the trauma, negative cognitions (thoughts) and mood (feelings) associated with the trauma, and an unhealthy, high level of arousal (such as hypervigilance, problems with concentration, and sleep disturbance). The aftereffects of complex trauma are a combination of those that follow trauma and additional issues that follow complex trauma, which include affect or emotional dysregulation, insecure adult attachment, negative self-concept, and difficulty learning from life. These aftereffects are discussed in the sections that follow.

Affect or Emotional Dysregulation

"Affect" is a term psychologists use for emotion; "affect dysregulation" is the term for severe problems in regulating emotions. "Regulating emotions" is the term for all the ways in which we understand, respond to, and modify our emotions. Our emotions come about sometimes because of external events. For example, we may experience a bereavement and feel sad, lonely, depressed, angry, and hopeless. Or an unwelcome life transition, such as divorce, brings us feelings of rage, helplessness, bitterness, depression, and revenge. Other times we experience emotions after internal events. We recall memories, we imagine future scenarios, we place interpretations on our interactions with others, or we find ourselves thinking about a past failure.

When these emotions occur, we need to decide what to do about both the emotions and the event that brought them about. Is there a response we should be making? Do we need to plan out a series of actions? Is our goal to fix a problem, to manage emotions, or both? Our responses are helped or hindered by the same emotions that created the need for a response. Our responses are helped if we keep our emotions at a level that does not interfere with our planning, but our responses are hindered or complicated if our emotions are so uncontrollable and intense that we are prevented from planning or acting.

Emotional regulation thus is not always about having positive emotions. Although positive emotions are good for our mental health, a normal life presents us with many occasions that call up negative emotions. The complex trauma aftereffect of emotional dysregulation means that adult survivors have learned only a few ways to respond to negative emotions, and most of those ways are unhelpful. For example, *rumination* is literally "chewing" the bad emotions and experiences, over and over, without any escape from those thoughts and with increasing self-blame. *Suppression* of negative emotions is the active avoidance of any aspect of the emotion, usually by numbing the feeling. Suppression by drugs or alcohol can lead to problems with addiction. But suppression can occur in other ways, such as acting out or engaging in risky behaviors or doing things that provide short-term rewards, such as compulsive shopping or gambling.

Complex trauma damages emotional regulation in several ways. First, heightened emotional reactivity means that we are especially sensitive to emotions and cannot stop reacting. Second, dissociation is a way that children cope with abuse, separating themselves during the event and seeing it from a distance; this helped us survive the terrible emotions of sexual abuse, but as adults, we use dissociation as a way of numbing our emotions, which prevents us from resolving them. Third, we may experience outbursts of anger or rage, which can occur without our having any control over them. Finally, reckless self-destructive behavior may help us numb our emotions, but it does not change them and often creates new problems.

Insecure Adult Attachment

The term *attachment* means connection to another person. For children, people who are "attachment figures" are normally parents, close family, and parentlike figures such as grandparents. Attachment is a biologically based system for finding help in facing threat or danger. When people "activate the attachment system," they seek the presence or help of attachment figures, which reduces their distress. People who are securely attached have repeated experiences of threat, help seeking, and reward. Even if the experience is difficult or dangerous, attachment experiences of the past reassure the person that others are available for help.

Childhood sexual abuse survivors have had multiple experiences with insecurity and failure of the threat–help seeking–reward sequence because their caregivers either abused them or did not protect them. The child then either tries desperately to receive help and caring from the caregiver or gives up trying. Because the child's brain continues to develop through adolescence, the child experiences especially strong "programming" of interpersonal failure and thus learns that no interpersonal relationship will be a source of caring and safety and that they are to blame for this outcome.

There are three attachment styles that start in childhood and continue into adulthood. The first style is called *insecure ambivalent*. This style develops as a child grows up with a caregiver who is inconsistent, who sometimes provides a caring response and sometimes is neglectful or hurtful. This child grows up to be dependent on others and suffers from fears of abandonment. The second style is *insecure avoidant*. This style develops as a child grows up with a distant and unengaged caregiver. As an adult, this person avoids closeness and dismisses the importance of their own and others' emotions. The third style is *disorganized*. This child experiences a caregiving environment that is abusive and chaotic. The caregiver is a source of fear, and the child learns to seek closeness from people they are afraid of. As adults, people with this style rely on impulsive responses (such as self-harm) to manage their emotions. Insights From Psychology 2.1 describes a study of childhood sexual abuse and relationship difficulties as adults.

Negative Self-Concept

During the developmental tasks of childhood, one desired outcome is that the child develops good feelings about the self. Psychologists use the term *self-concept* to mean the beliefs and feelings a person has about their physical, emotional, spiritual, and intellectual self. No one has completely positive views of the self; that is itself unrealistic and is a problem in self-concept. But a healthy self-concept belongs to a person who has self-esteem (that is, thinks realistically well of himself or herself), a positive self-image (that is, believes he or she is usually seen by others favorably), and a healthy ideal self (that is, has goals for improving the self in the future and sees those goals as attainable).

Children who are sexually abused, however, believe that they are responsible for the abuse because of who they are, or what they did, or what they failed to do. The feeling that they are and always will be bad or wrong and therefore are defeated and worthless stays into adulthood. Because this feeling was created by the self, even positive experiences of success do not alter this negative self-concept.

Difficulty Learning From Life

Another way of thinking about the consequences of complex trauma has to do with how the survivor interacts with and learns from life. This process begins with the abused child living in a situation of adversity. "Adversity" means great difficulty. Children who are

Insights From Psychology 2.1

Is Childhood Sexual Abuse Related to Difficulties in Adult Romantic Relationships?

The experiences of children in the caregiving they receive influence the expectations they have for romantic relationships as adults. Because childhood sexual abuse usually happens in relationships a child has with a family member, close friend, or trusted adult, the child fails to experience "secure attachment"—psychological safety and security in the relationships that matter the most to them. As adults, insecure attachment influences their experience with intimate romantic relationships.

A group of psychologists interviewed two groups of women at two points in time (Lassri et al., 2018). One group had been sexually abused as children by a family member, and the other group had not been abused. The participants gave information on their levels of distress, self-criticism, and attachment and on their satisfaction with their current romantic relationship. The results of the study showed that the women who had been abused were significantly less satisfied with their relationships. This was likely for two reasons. First, they were more self-critical than the non-abused group, which had led to problems in their romantic relationships. Second, the abused women were more avoidant in their attachment styles, meaning that they felt vulnerable and uncomfortable in interpersonal relationships, including their romantic relationship.

The connection between childhood sexual abuse and later difficulties in adult interpersonal relationships is well established. This study was helpful in understanding adult relationships by revealing the important influence of self-criticism. In Chapter 1, I discussed how abuse can lead to blaming the self and then to guilt and shame. When the child turns those feelings inward, he or she becomes self-critical. As adults, people who are excessively self-critical are difficult relationship partners; they take everything personally, they get overly defensive when criticized, they procrastinate. This study suggests there is a vicious cycle in which self-criticism leads to difficulties in romantic relationships, which in turn lead to more self-criticism and blaming, which lead to greater dissatisfaction, as well as more unsatisfying relationships in the future.

53

securely attached to their caregivers turn to them in times of need and stress. But abused children do not experience security in their attachment relationships. Therefore, they are especially vulnerable to stress and adversity because of their expectation that no one will be there for help.

In our everyday interactions with the external and internal environments, our thoughts typically are relatively slow, controlled, and flexible. When a threat (stimulus) appears, we switch to rapid, automatic, and tightly focused thinking (response). Recall the fight-or-flight response: Our body experiences a series of internal changes that power our response to the threat. Additionally, under normal circumstances, we learn from the threat. Most important, we use other people to "process," or talk about and think through, the threat, and that conversation creates an opportunity to learn about the self (what happened inside us) and the environment (what happened outside of us—how the threat unfolded in the environment). Insights From Psychology 2.2 explains research on how childhood sexual abuse might affect being able to understand the feelings of others.

In summary, the concept of complex trauma is a better match for the experiences and aftereffects of childhood sexual abuse. This is so for several reasons:

- The sexual abuse of a child betrays a relationship that should provide nurturance, support, learning, care, and love.
- That betrayal leads the child to modes of being that initially protect the child but that continue into adulthood, where they create new problems.
- Complex trauma is the experience of repeated, prolonged adversity during childhood, usually within a caregiving relationship.
- Complex trauma leads to the consequences of trauma and the additional consequences of complex trauma. The consequences of trauma include experiencing repeated and unwanted

Insights From Psychology 2.2

Are You Angry at Me? The Effect of Childhood Sexual Abuse on Seeing Contempt and Anger in Others

One of the developmental tasks in childhood is learning to understand the feelings of others, a quality called "empathy." We use various cues to understand how someone else is feeling. Those cues might be the content of their language and its tone, or nonverbal cues such as facial expression and posture. The child is in a learning mode during interactions as they practice accurately assessing the feelings of the other while also being in tune with their own feelings. Being able to reflect on and understand feelings lets the child relate what is going on in the present situation to past experiences. Childhood sexual abuse denies the child the context and opportunity to be themselves in a relationship and to learn to interpret others' feelings from caring and supportive people.

A study by a group of psychologists tested three groups of adults: One group had experienced trauma as adults, one group had experienced childhood abuse, and one group had not experienced trauma (Pfaltz et al., 2019). All of the participants watched 300 short film segments showing actors with facial emotions that were neutral or that displayed one of nine specific emotions (for example, anger or joy). The goal of the study was to determine how accurately the three groups labeled the emotions and how they responded to the neutral facial expressions.

The findings revealed that the three groups were equally accurate in labeling the specific emotions shown by the actors. But the adults who were abused as children differed from the other two groups in their assessment of the neutral facial emotions. They saw the neutral expressions more often as contempt or anger. The researchers proposed that people who were abused as children learned to associate a neutral facial expression with threat, rather than a neutral or calm feeling, and developed hypervigilance that caused them to misinterpret neutrality as anger or as contempt.

The researchers concluded that children may learn negative interpretations of neutral facial expressions during their mistreatment. These negative interpretations might be helpful in the child's environment by signaling threat, but in adulthood they interfere with empathic understanding of others and with building interpersonal relationships.

intrusions of dreams or images of the trauma, avoiding any cue related to the trauma, and having a constant sense of threat (being "jumpy" all the time). Complex trauma adds the consequences of having emotional dysregulation, with either extra-strong or numbed emotions; believing you are defeated and worthless; and feeling distant and isolated from other people, including those with whom you want to be in a relationship.

INCEST AND THE CHILD'S BEREAVEMENT

Incest is sexual contact between close family members. In the case of childhood sexual abuse, incest occurs between a child and his or her father, mother, stepparent, sibling or stepsibling, uncle, aunt, or grandparent. It is not necessary for the sexual contact to involve intercourse; the same range of sexual and sexualized behaviors as in childhood sexual abuse also constitute incest. And the same over-arching description applies: The child is exploited by an older person for that person's sexual desires, and the child is unable to consent because of their age and developmental stage and their dependence on the familial relationship.

Affection-based incest serves as a way for the perpetrator to give and receive affection. The child may be treated as "special" by the perpetrator; an example is when the perpetrator routinely gives the child gifts that the other children in the family (or the other parent) do not receive. Erotic-based incest occurs in families that are overly sexualized. Sometimes multiple family members are involved. Aggression-based incest is a way for the perpetrator to deal with frustrations and blockages in their life. The incest is an expression of the hostility felt by the perpetrator, and sexual activities may involve some degree of physical abuse as well. Rage-based incest usually is accompanied by physical abuse, even sadism, and is especially dangerous for the victim.

It is a misunderstanding of incest to believe it occurs only in "chaotic" families. A chaotic family is disorganized, has difficulties meeting basic needs such as food and shelter, experiences frequent coming and going of people such as a parent's romantic partners, and may be involved with social services and law enforcement.

The children in a chaotic family must fend for themselves and meet their own physical and emotional needs, and their vulnerability leads them to a higher risk of abuse by people within and outside the family. But incest occurs as often within normal-appearing families. This type of family seems from the outside to be stable and well-adjusted. There are obvious financial resources. The adults hold responsible jobs, and the children seem to be successful at school and in activities. The family may be involved members of a religious community. But the family, inside the deceptive appearance, suffer from the same problems as the chaotic family.

Although incest survivors are also childhood sexual abuse survivors, their adult experience has some distinct characteristics. First, they may experience "emotional incontinence": They cannot limit or stop the distressing feelings. Second, they may engage in dysfunctional self-soothing; because normal means of self-soothing (such as calming oneself, using activity as a distraction, or receiving support from others) were not possible, they manage their emotions by using addictive substances or self-harm rituals. Third, they may convert emotional problems to physical symptoms without recognizing their connection. Fourth, they may experience sexual dysfunction; they may be inhibited or engage in compulsive reenactment. Finally, they often experience failures of relatedness: They try to please or be inoffensive to others while mistrusting them.

Earlier, we discussed the contribution to our understanding of childhood sexual abuse by adding on the concept of complex trauma. Trauma leads to threat and fear; complex trauma leads to fear and shame. A necessary additional concept for understanding incest is the experience of loss.

Incest creates devastating losses for the child, including loss of control, loss of innocence, and loss of safety. One of the most overwhelming losses is that of possible selves (Markus & Nurius, 1986). "Possible selves" are who we desire to be, who we might become, and who we fear becoming. Incest destroys many possible selves for the child, and later the adult; who we desire to be may never be possible because of our life experiences. For many survivors, the experience of incest changed their lives forever, and that experience sets them apart from others in ways that cannot be explained.

Another loss is the loss of true mourning. Incest is not the death of a person, but it creates many smaller deaths in the child and later the adult. For example, the adult may mourn the loss of the healthy relationship they were denied as a child. But those losses are ambiguous; they may not feel as "real" as an actual death. How does the adult grieve the loss of the innocent child? This concept makes sense to the adult survivor, but how exactly is that done? There is no grave to visit, no service to attend. And yet the loss is very great, and grieving must occur.

An additional loss is experienced as the inability to control past circumstances. As later chapters describe, the adult must confront a variety of difficulties in his or her present life. But it will always be impossible to change the past. As the present comes under more scrutiny, the past is also reexperienced and seen in a new way. But the essential facts remain, and there is much grief that attaches to those hard realities.

In some families, the child experiences "covert incest." Covert incest occurs when the child becomes the close, even intimate, partner of a parent. There is no sexual activity per se, but the interactions have a sexual overtone. For example, the parent may use the child as a "date" for an event, or make lewd comments to the child, such as "You have a nice ass." The parent may violate physical boundaries in touching the child, or personal boundaries, such as commenting on the child's physical progress through puberty. The child feels trapped in the relationship with the parent and knows the relationship is not right, and in fact feels "icky." The concept of enmeshment is often applicable to families with covert incest. *Enmeshment* occurs when appropriate and necessary physical and emotional boundaries are ignored or violated. The enmeshment continues into adulthood when the parent ignores or belittles the adult child or violates a boundary. For example, the parent wants to know everything about the child, including information the parent does not need to know. The parent's self-worth is centered on the child's accomplishments. The child is criticized if they want less contact (such as not seeing the parent every weekend) or if they make a choice that is good for themselves (such as changing jobs or locations). And the child believes it is their job to make everyone in the family happy.

After experiencing covert incest, the adult child's primary need is to set and maintain boundaries. Boundaries can be physical, as in wanting privacy or not wanting someone to touch their body. They can be role boundaries: I am responsible for doing this, and you are responsible for doing that. The adult child is able to set emotional boundaries when they believe they have the right to their feelings, the right to be treated with respect, and the right to withdraw from interacting with a person who treats them badly. (If the concept of boundaries is new to you, there are resources at the end of the chapter for more information on this topic.)

FINDING A NEW PATH FORWARD

I know this chapter contains information that is hard and has "sharp corners." I hope that knowing why you feel as you do, and how your life came to be where it is today, is helpful to you. In the chapters ahead, I will describe the pathways that will help you move forward. You are a victim of what was done to you, but you do not need to stay one. The goal of this book is to help you take steps along a pathway forward and, in so doing, learn to thrive.

RESOURCES

Digital Resources

- The National Child Traumatic Stress Network (https://www. nctsn.org) was created by Congress in 2000 to provide services to children and their families after childhood trauma. The website offers resources for people such as teachers who work with children, for the families of children suffering trauma, and for survivors.
- Bring Change to Mind (https://bringchange2mind.org) is a nonprofit organization devoted to reducing stigma and discrimination around mental illness. It was founded by actress Glenn Close in 2010 after two family members were diagnosed with mental illnesses. The website has resources (including a blog) and many stories from survivors.

Print Resources

- *Finding Life Beyond Trauma: Using Acceptance and Commitment Therapy to Heal From Post-Traumatic Stress and Trauma-Related Problems*, by Victoria M. Follette and Jacqueline Pistorello (New Harbinger, 2007). This workbook offers information and exercises to help survivors of trauma accept the past, heal from it, and live a more fulfilling life. The information is relevant to all trauma but is especially helpful for childhood sexual abuse.

- *It's Not You, It's What Happened to You: Complex Trauma and Treatment*, by Christine Courtois (Telemachus Press, 2014). The author is widely known among psychologists for her work with survivors and her contributions to the study of complex trauma. This book discusses trauma and complex trauma and describes trauma-related problems such as distressing emotions and invasive memories.

- *REPAIR Your Life: A Program for Recovery From Incest and Childhood Sexual Abuse*, by Marjorie McKinnon (Loving Healing Press, 2016). This book outlines a program for repair, with stages corresponding to each letter of "REPAIR." For example, I stands for Insight: seeing accurately your experiences and what "rules" they created in you. There are exercises and descriptions for each stage.

- *The Complex PTSD Workbook: A Mind–Body Approach to Regaining Emotional Control and Becoming Whole*, by Arielle Schwartz (Althea Press, 2016). Just as PTSD can follow trauma, complex PTSD can follow complex trauma. This workbook focuses on changing avoidance symptoms, invasive symptoms, and depressive symptoms and provides information and exercises.

- *Trauma Survivors' Strategies for Healing: A Workbook to Help You Grow, Rebuild, and Take Back Your Life*, by Elena Welsh (Althea Press, 2018). This workbook addresses difficulties faced by survivors in the broad categories of emotions, thoughts, the body, and relationships. There are many exercises and self-assessments and space for journaling in the book.

CHAPTER 3

RECOVERY

Recovery Milestones

This chapter will help you

1. **identify** tasks of recovery,
2. **define** specific signs professional help might be useful or needed during recovery, and
3. **find out** your personal strengths.

I enjoy listening to a band, Switchfoot, that reminds me of music that was popular when I was a young adult. Their music is indie rock, their lyrics are dark, and they refer to their style as "music for thinking people." I love the band's name, and I see it as a picture of recovery. The band members are surfers, and to surf "switch" or "switch footed" is to ride with the foot forward that is opposite from one's natural stance. You are probably used to living life with your dominant foot forward. But switching to the other foot, to new ways of being, is the beginning of your recovery, even though it will feel difficult, just as using the less-dominant foot is more difficult.

This chapter is a bridge between the first two chapters, which provide facts about childhood sexual abuse and complex trauma, and the next seven chapters, which introduce you to resources for the recovery journey, as well as the last chapter, which introduces you to thriving. Again, you may be reading this chapter without having read the first two, so brief summaries of previous content are provided. And headings let you choose what to read about and in what order. Helping you move from being a victim to surviving to thriving is the goal of this book. This chapter begins that journey by giving you foundational knowledge about yourself and your strengths.

WHAT IS THE SELF?

The question of recovery—What is recovery?—has another question inside of it: Who is recovering? Who is it, exactly, that is locked inside of your traumatic memory? Chapters 1 and 2 described how the brain's capacity for processing information can be overwhelmed by traumatic memory. Because you were a child, your beliefs about your abuse created a kind of prison that you could not escape or talk yourself out of. Knowing how your self functions, and how it was damaged, begins your recovery.

Psychologists historically saw the self as a container of everything that came at it. For example, the self could be defined by developmental stages—childhood, adolescence, adulthood, and so on. Psychologists viewed young people one way, older people another. Or the self could be a set of personality traits created by nature (inherited genes) and nurture (environment). Or the self could be the totality of the individual's interactions with the environment, where interactions that were rewarding and those that were punishing made the self what it is. So a child who grew up in poverty but with supportive parents might be viewed as a mix of those two factors. But all these self-representations are passive: The self is at the mercy of something else.

The better view, and the more contemporary view, is that the self is *dynamic*—that is, active and forceful. The self acts on our external environment—the world around us. It changes in response to our internal environment—our plans or hopes or fears. And it is multidimensional: The self-concept is not a unitary thing, but rather consists of different "selves." So, for example, I might think of myself as a good teacher but a bad parent. Additionally, we describe ourselves to ourselves or to others using concepts we can think about—self-representations. In other words, we think about how we see ourselves. This aspect of your self is very important in recovery.

Self-Representations

Self-representations are images, theories, beliefs, self-evaluations, assumptions, and more that make up our selves. But self-representations differ from one another in three key ways:

1. *Importance:* Self-representations differ in how important they are to us. If you think about all that makes up "you," some of those building blocks are much more important—they are central to your idea of you—whereas others are peripheral, and you use them only occasionally.

2. *Presence:* We experience some self-representations as reflecting our current sense of self. Others reflect who we were, or who we are in the process of becoming. Still others might reflect selves we hope for or fear becoming in the future. Selves that do not currently exist—possible selves—have a strong influence on our lives.

3. *Value:* Self-representations can be generally positive, or generally negative, or a combination of the two. We think of "bad me" with negative self-representations. And we think of "good me," even if dimly, with positive self-representations.

The self is a very large group of self-representations that are not all working at the same time. The "working self-concept" is the one that is operating in the moment, the "continually active, shifting array of accessible self-knowledge" (Markus & Wurf, 1987, p. 306). An *array* is a set of things; think of your self-representations as an array of words on a page that form a word picture. All those words are in your self-concept, but only some of them are activated, or turned on, at any point in time. What makes this array change are shifts in our external environments, or our internal environments, or both. Think of one self-representation you have right now that seems most active or influential to you today: Was that part of your self as active a month ago? a year ago?

Where do self-representations, the building blocks of the self, come from? Psychologists believe there are four sources. First, we build self-representations by observing ourselves. Our own experiences influence how we see ourselves. Second, we make direct attempts to understand ourselves. Have you ever filled out a personality questionnaire online? We want an "objective" way of seeing ourselves. Third, we compare ourselves to other people. This, too, is common, and psychologists call this process "social comparison." I may not be as talented as my friend Wendy in do-it-yourself projects, but I am a more confident bread baker than my friend Susan. The fourth source is our social environment; in other words, we get direct information from others about how they see us.

As we recover, what roles does our self play? One role is to give us continuity. We exist in time and space while our self builds a story that links our past, present, and future. Another role of our self is to make us sensitive to information in our environment. We cannot pay attention to everything in our environment, but the self picks out some points and ignores others. Still another role of our self is to be a motivating personal trainer. This desired function of the self changes vague ideas into concrete plans. When you have a strong sense of self, you feel good about the person you are now and are becoming. You maintain your integrity and your sense of being whole. And you stay focused on your goals.

Possible Selves

Possible selves are in our future. "Possible selves" are the selves we want to become, the selves we might become, and the selves we want to avoid or are afraid of becoming. Possible selves are not just vague ideas but rather specific, personally relevant selves. Possible selves are plans for what is possible and what we desire. They direct us to tasks we need to master, and they give us a road map for the future. How does childhood sexual abuse damage our possible selves? Possible selves partially come about from past selves, especially when those past selves are images we want to avoid in the future. We know that complex trauma harms our self during childhood at a time when the self should be growing and expanding. Because systems that filter incoming information are damaged by our trauma experience, only information that agrees with our negative view of ourselves comes in. Thus, we find it hard to have positive possible selves.

The journey of recovery begins when you start to see positive possible selves and learn to rely on them. It is true that your past selves remain to a certain degree, and you'll carry them with you into recovery. But by selecting specific possible selves you wish to journey toward, you actively build your future. Self-Assessment 3.1 is an exercise to help you think about all of your selves, including your possible selves.

Self-Compassion

Thinking about yourself may have shown you that you are a harsh critic of yourself. This is common with survivors because we find our actions and our characteristics to be flawed. There is an idea in psychology, defined by psychologist Kristen Neff (2003), that is associated with many mental health benefits—self-compassion. Neff's website (https://www.self-compassion.org) contains information about

Self-Assessment 3.1

Your Selves

Directions: In your journal, or whatever note-taking app you like to use, write your answers to these questions about selves. It doesn't matter how much or how little you write. This assessment is meant to help you identify selves and see how they influence recovery.

1. Think about your *past selves*. Seeing your past selves as pictures might be easier than naming or describing them. Here is a past self I identified for me that may help you: a lost, abandoned child frozen in the snow. This helps my recovery by telling me how I experienced my abuse—as being frozen in place. Maybe I am frozen in place still. What past selves can you identify now?

2. Think about your *current selves*. Here is a current self I identified for me: an outward achiever with a hidden dark side. This helps my recovery by telling me that I have parts of myself that are not working together, but rather working in different directions. Knowing that gives me a recovery goal of helping integrate parts of myself. What current selves can you identify now?

3. Think about your *possible selves*. Here is a possible self for me: someone who is no longer afraid. Knowing that helps my recovery by showing me that fear is going to be important to recognize and act against. What possible selves you can think of?

4. What are you most proud of right now?

5. What would you not ever change about yourself?

Do the answers to these last two questions help you identify more possible selves? If so, add them to your previous list.

Write out a few sentences about yourself using what you learned in this assessment. For example, if your possible self is like mine—no longer afraid—ask yourself, what does not being afraid look like as I move through a day? How do I move through the world if I am not afraid? If you wish, use an online program such as https://wordclouds.com to make a word picture of your selves.

self-compassion and a test to determine how self-compassionate you are. It would be helpful if you take that test now or soon; it will give you scores on parts of self-compassion and their opposites, as well as a total score. Self-compassion involves three parts. The first is self-kindness. When you are kind to yourself, you give yourself positive support and reduce harsh self-criticism. Self-kindness includes accepting the fact that imperfection, mistakes, and even failure are inevitable and, in fact, a daily occurrence. The second part is connection or common humanity. Connection depends on recognizing and accepting that imperfection is a common human experience. You do not have to isolate yourself or withdraw when you make mistakes or fail. The third part of self-compassion is mindfulness. With mindfulness, you can hold negative thoughts and emotions gently; you do not become one with them or automatically suppress them. Being mindful does not mean always having positive emotions. Rather, you can "sit next to" all your emotions, positive and negative, in a way that acknowledges them but without being overwhelmed by them.

Being self-compassionate is linked to improved psychological well-being, including reduced depression and anxiety. These benefits of self-compassion have been demonstrated among adults as well as other groups, including adolescents, older adults, and people with chronic diseases. Self-compassion operates on several "channels," one of which is physiological; self-compassion has been linked to decreases in heart rate and increases in the hormone oxytocin, which promotes interpersonal attachment (for example, mother–child bonding). Insights From Psychology 3.1 describes a study of how increasing their self-compassion helped women who had experienced a negative event reduce binge eating during low moods.

Is there a set amount of self-compassion? Do people just have more or less of it? Or is it a skill you can learn? Thankfully, research has shown that you can improve your self-compassion. Several of

Insights From Psychology 3.1

Self-Compassion and Binge Eating

Many survivors soothe themselves through binge eating. *Binge eating* is eating large quantities of food in a short amount of time without being able to control it. People who do this frequently are self-critical and experience shame after a binge episode. They believe that criticizing themselves will help them avoid this harmful behavior in the future. The problem is that self-criticism does not change the behavior, but only increases their feelings of shame and inferiority.

A recent study by psychologists Lucy Serpell, Rebecca Amey, and Sunjeev Kamboj (2020) examined how self-criticism and self-compassion influence eating behaviors after a negative event. The researchers selected 60 women with symptoms of disordered eating (binge eating or bulimia) to participate in the study. The women did a word-finding problem and then were given false negative feedback; they were told they did poorly, no matter what their actual performance was. After this feedback, which was shown to increase their negative mood and decrease their positive mood, the women received instructions on how to give themselves either self-compassionate feedback or self-critical feedback on the word-finding problem. Next, the women were given food (chocolate, muffins, cookies) and asked to sample the food, rate how pleasant they found it, and then eat as much as they wished.

The women who received the self-compassion instructions behaved differently than the women who received the self-critical instructions. Those who used self-compassion saw the food as less pleasant and ate less of it when it was freely available than those who were self-critical. Previous research had shown that negative emotions such as anxiety or shame damage the sense of control over one's eating, and this study found that self-compassion can reduce the feelings that result in broken self-regulation. The finding that the instructions to be self-compassionate improved the women's control over their eating (unlike the instructions to be self-critical) shows how important it is to increase your self-compassion.

the handbooks listed at the end of this chapter contain exercises with that goal. In support of the assertion that self-compassion can be improved, Ferrari and colleagues (2019) analyzed 27 published studies covering 1,400 participants who received treatments to increase their self-compassion. The authors documented that participants who received self-compassion interventions showed increased self-compassion, decreased negative emotions (such as depression), reduced self-criticism and rumination, and lowered stress.

To summarize, here is what we know about the self:

- Our self is not a simple container of everything that we experience, but rather is an active and dynamic entity.
- We build our selves with self-representations, which are images, theories, or ideas about ourselves.
- These self-representations differ from one another; for example, some are more important to us than others, and some are positive and some negative.
- As survivors, we experienced abuse that damaged our self. Thus, we need to think about ourselves in new ways and identify possible selves that help us set goals for our future.
- Self-compassion is a powerful way of relating to ourselves in a noncritical, humane way that sees our failures as a normal part of human life.

WHAT IS RECOVERY?

What is *recovery*? The word in its original use meant to get back something that had been lost or stolen. An additional meaning is used in health care; recovery is the return to "normal" or the state that applied before disease or injury took hold. Although *illness* is defined as the presence of symptoms that signal a problem in the body's functioning, is recovery merely the absence of those symptoms? Is "health" the same as "not illness," or is it more? Our own experience and the work of many scientists and scholars tell us that health is more than simply "not ill." In the same way, recovery is more than just reversing the past.

A synthesis of the tasks that make up recovery was outlined by Leamy and colleagues (2011) and can be easily recalled by the acronym CHIME. Here are the tasks you accomplish as you recover from your childhood abuse:

- You establish *Connectedness*. Isolation does not help recovery because it removes us from care and support provided by other people. Most forms of recovery, such as 12-step recovery models, value the presence of a community of other individuals who are recovering.

- You establish *Hope and optimism* about your future. For recovery to happen, you believe in change, you see new possible selves, and you use resources to fight against factors working to keep you down and discouraged. As you'll see in Chapter 10, hope is much more than a wish or a desire; it includes concrete plans.

- You establish a new *Identity*. For many years, my first waking thought was about the abuse I suffered. It was a slow process for my identity to be more than the abuse. Eventually, I built a new identity as I explored who I was and who I wanted to be. My new identity has the power to redefine my life.

- You discover and create *Meaning and purpose* in all you do. Meaning permeates all aspects of your life from your past to your future, including your spirituality and your roles. And your new meaning is so solid that a return to your meaningless past is impossible.

- You build *Empowerment*. Empowerment increases your stamina—your capacity for prolonged physical and mental effort. Empowerment gives you control over your responses to circumstances and to situations. Empowerment rests on a clear vision of your strengths.

Using Professional Help

As Chapter 2 explained, the experience of complex trauma creates difficulties that persist into adult life. If you did not read that section, here I describe difficulties you might be having. One is reexperiencing: There might be times when it feels like the abuse is happening again, and you might have flashbacks or nightmares or extreme physical reactions when reminded of the trauma. Another is avoidance: Survivors use a lot of energy to avoid all aspects of the abuse, such as by not thinking or talking about it, numbing themselves using drugs or alcohol, or avoiding reminders such as people or locations. A third is sense of threat: You might be super vigilant or watchful, or you might feel nervous or jumpy all the time. Another difficulty is managing or regulating your emotions (called "affect dysregulation"): You might experience your emotions as a problem, either because you have too much of them and are overwhelmed, or because you feel like you have no feelings (which might lead you to harm yourself). The last difficulty is negative self-concept: You might feel defeated, worthless, dirty, contaminated, or guilty.

As you recover, you should consider when professional help would be useful. Here are several reasons that getting help might be a good choice. First, providers are trained to be a special presence in your life. They respect you, and they listen without judgment. Second, providers have learned how to use certain strategies in their interactions with you. For example, one strategy is education, which they might use to give you helpful information about abuse or your reactions to it. Another strategy is to give you specific coping methods to reduce the difficulties you are experiencing because of complex trauma.

Getting professional help is necessary, rather than only a consideration, when your life is sending you certain signals. Here is a list of these signals from the U.S. government agency in charge of reducing substance abuse and improving mental health (Substance Abuse and Mental Health Services Administration, 2014):

- You are very unstable in your environment, whether that is a physical location or a social network or an employment network; in other words, you don't know from day to day what will happen and therefore can't plan or cope.
- You experienced a recent traumatic event, perhaps a revictimization, that caused you great distress.
- You use self-harm for coping (such as cutting or risky behaviors).
- You have thought about suicide and have a plan.
- You use drugs or alcohol far too much.
- You have "dissociative symptoms," which include periods of lost time, feelings that you are not present some of the time, and lapses in memory.

Probably the clearest signal that you need to talk with someone is suicidal thoughts. If you have been thinking about suicide, there are resources that can help you right away. By calling the national suicide hotline at 1-800-273-8255, you can tell a counselor what you're going through. Or you can text TALK to 741-741, a crisis text line. You can also call the Rape, Abuse, and Incest National Network, or RAINN, at 1-800-656-HOPE (4673), or chat with a counselor online at https://www.rainn.org.

Several types of providers work with people who have experienced complex trauma. The differences among providers have to do with years of training (after the undergraduate degree), the specific foundation of their training, the skills they possess, and the treatments they offer. Psychiatrists have earned an MD degree; they have completed medical school, a residency, and a fellowship. Psychiatrists prescribe medications, and some have training in psychological treatments for trauma. Psychologists have completed a PhD or PsyD degree followed by an internship and a residency. They offer psychological treatments, and some states give them the authority to prescribe medications. Two types of provider have earned master's degrees: social workers (MSW) and mental health counselors (MS or MA); both offer psychological treatments. Finally, nurse practitioners who have MSN degrees can receive training that enables them to prescribe and deliver psychological treatments.

How do you choose a provider? One place to begin is to get a referral from your primary care provider; another is to check with the state association or networks of providers to find suggestions. You can learn about potential providers from their websites, which typically include information to help you decide whether that provider is a good match for you. Few providers leave their training programs with expertise on complex trauma, so check to see whether a provider you're considering has had special training in trauma. In addition, you'll need to determine how to pay for services. You can consult your health insurance to determine coverage you have for psychological services or consider low-cost and no-cost community mental health services. Once you've located a provider who looks promising, schedule a "get acquainted" appointment. By the end of that appointment, you should feel comfortable working with the provider and have confidence in the treatment plan they propose.

Focusing on Your Strengths

When you are focused on what is wrong with your life, it can feel odd to read about strengths. Shouldn't you try to reduce your weaknesses? For many years, psychology agreed with that view, in the belief that what was needed for improved mental health was to "treat" what was "wrong" with people. This view is termed the "medical model" or the "disease model" because it is the model used in medicine. You go to the doctor or other health care provider with a set of symptoms, which are signs that something is wrong. You are diagnosed on the basis of those symptoms and given a treatment to make you well. That treatment usually takes the symptoms away.

A different model, positive psychology, was introduced to the psychology field in 2000 (Seligman & Csikszentmihalyi, 2000). *Positive psychology* is the study of "strengths and virtues" rather than the study of "weaknesses and damages." Positive psychologists have identified characteristics that lead to better lives even for people who have great difficulties. People are more than their burdens: Everyone wants to live lives that are satisfying and joyful and to have accomplishments that bring happiness and engagement.

What makes for a good life? If you believe that a good life gives you pleasure, you endorse a "hedonic" viewpoint. *Hedonism* is the belief that only pleasure has worth or value. In contrast to that belief is a "eudaemonic" viewpoint; *eudaemonia* is the belief that a good life gives you meaning. Psychologist Carol Ryff (1989) described a meaningful life as one that has the following:

- *Self-acceptance:* When you are self-accepting, you accept both "good" and "bad" qualities in yourself. When you are not self-accepting, you do not like yourself, and you yearn to be different.
- *Personal growth:* Having a mindset oriented to personal growth means you are open to new experiences and to challenges in your life. Having a mindset oriented away from personal growth means that you have given up on making changes or improvements, and you may feel trapped.
- *Purpose in life:* Seeing your life as meaningful and having goals for the future provide a high level of purpose in life. Believing

that your life has no direction and is essentially meaningless indicates a low level of purpose in life.

* *Positive relationships with others:* Having positive interpersonal relationships does not mean having lots of friends. Rather, it means that the friendships and social connections you do have are mutual and trusting.

* *Mastery:* Mastery means feeling competent and capable of solving problems and making decisions. If you feel out of control and are always reacting to events outside yourself, you have lower mastery.

* *Autonomy:* Autonomy means having a strong sense of yourself: your beliefs, your values, your standards. If you feel pressured by others and cannot decide or act on your own beliefs and values, you have low autonomy.

"Positive psychology" does not see life as always positive or recommend thinking only "positive thoughts." People who criticize positive psychology for these reasons have not learned about what it truly is. Difficulties, even traumas, occur, and people's well-being is damaged. But positive psychologists believe that people can bring about good outcomes even in the presence of challenge and despair. The virtues and strengths emphasized by positive psychologists are common across cultures and across history; they are qualities that have always been associated with well-being. Self-Assessment 3.2 gives you the opportunity to learn about your own virtues and strengths.

Recovery can occur after trauma. When that happens, psychologists use the term *posttraumatic growth*. Posttraumatic growth occurs when you emerge from trauma with sustained personal growth in one or more areas of life. Tedeschi and Calhoun (2004), two psychologists, examined the evidence for posttraumatic growth and defined specific areas of life in which this growth can occur. One area of growth they found is changes in how people see themselves.

Self-Assessment 3.2

What Are Your Strengths?

This assessment is meant to help you identify your personal strengths and begin to see how they might be useful in your recovery. Take the free survey of strengths found at https://www.viacharacter.org/character-strengths. Then, using your journal or note-taking app, write out, for each of the following six categories, one or two strengths you see in yourself, along with an example of how you showed each strength in the past year:

1. *Wisdom and knowledge:* Strengths that help you obtain and use knowledge (creativity, curiosity, open-mindedness, love of learning, perspective)
2. *Courage:* Strengths that help you accomplish a goal or a plan despite obstacles (bravery, persistence, integrity, vitality)
3. *Humanity:* Strengths that help you create relationships and partnerships with others (love, kindness, social intelligence)
4. *Justice:* Strengths that help the community (citizenship, fairness, leadership)
5. *Temperance:* Strengths that keep you from excess (forgiveness, humility, prudence, self-regulation)
6. *Transcendence:* Strengths that connect you with the larger universe (appreciation of beauty and excellence, gratitude, hope, humor, spirituality).

They might gain a better understanding of their own strengths, or develop the belief that they are stronger for having experienced the trauma. A second area of growth is a changed sense of relationship with others. People who experience growth after trauma report that they value interpersonal relationships in a new way. A changed philosophy of life is a third area of growth. After trauma, specific religious beliefs and practices may change or be left behind. But people often report a new sense of spirituality or a new commitment to their religion or faith. A fourth area is new possibilities. People might change their career or job goals, embrace new and different approaches to life, or have new interests. The last area of growth is greater appreciation of life. People recovering from trauma report a greater sense of gratitude, including for the "small things" in life. How does trauma create growth? This possibility seems contradictory to our own experience and to research on the negative effects of posttraumatic stress. Ronnie Janoff-Bulman (2004), a psychologist well known for her work on trauma, described how these positive outcomes can occur. One way to a positive outcome is strength through suffering: This is the "redemptive" view of personal difficulties, in which we become aware of previously undiscovered strengths and see ourselves differently only after our struggle. Another way to a positive outcome is psychological preparedness: In this view, our assumptions about the world being a safe place change, and we prepare for future trauma by learning from previously experienced trauma. A third way to a positive outcome after trauma is existential reevaluation: People are meaning makers, and creating personal meaning after being victimized is a critical contributor to our recovery.

In summary, here is what positive psychology contributes to recovery:

- Psychologists realize that focusing on what is "right" about people is necessary and important, in addition to focusing on what is "wrong."
- There are specific qualities—virtues and strengths—associated with living a life that is flourishing, meaningful, and satisfying.
- Posttraumatic growth has been demonstrated to occur to many people after trauma, and the ways in which this growth is developed and maintained are important to our recovery.

Telling Your Story as a Recovery Journey

You may not be telling your story to other people yet, but you tell your story to yourself. I end this chapter by asking you to tell your recovery story. But you don't need to tell your story to someone else or write out an autobiographical version. Instead, use your journal or note-taking app to complete the following exercise:

> You are going on a physical journey from where you are now to a place you wish to be.
>
> 1. Choose a **hero**. This is the main character in your story, and it could be you, or an animal, or a made-up person, or someone in a book or movie. What is the hero like?
> 2. Choose a physical **place** where your story starts, and describe this place. If you know the physical place where you hope to end up, describe that place as well.
> 3. Choose one or more **obstacles**, which could be villains or physical obstacles such as walls or rocks or a river. Describe the obstacles in your story. Are they obvious or hidden?
> 4. Choose **assets**—things to help you on your journey—which could be helpers or magical skills or tools. They might be strengths you have identified. What are the assets in your story?
> 5. Choose a **mood** for the story. What soundtrack is playing? What is the lighting like? What colors do you see?
> 6. Choose a **goal**. What is the hero seeking? Where is he or she going?

When I composed my first story, I told it to the counselor I was seeing at the time. It was a very simple story. It went something like this:

> The place was a village along a river. The village had a few houses and some trees. The river was blue and not too wide. It was summer. There were people in the village. And I was the hero, and I was in the village as a girl with her dog. I did not have any

assets, only my dog, who was enthusiastic for adventures. The obstacles were a group of soldiers who had come to the village in boats on the river. They were there to steal jewels the villagers had stored in chests. I wanted to be able to help the villagers, but I couldn't stop the soldiers from taking the jewels. I watched them load the chests into boats and paddle their boats away. This ending made me sad, because it seemed that no one could stop the soldiers.

This story is not elaborate, and yours may not be either. Later, my stories were more developed and had a new asset in the person of a magical wizard, and the dog turned out to be an asset, too. The soldiers reappeared in later stories, too; they were the villains.

When you begin a journey, you leave one place but are not yet at the intended destination. This concept might not disturb you if you left your house or apartment but haven't yet reached the grocery store. But for you, now, to leave what you know, but not be where you want to be, is ambiguous and probably makes you anxious. There is an interesting concept from sociology and anthropology called "liminality." Liminality is essentially the state of being in between. In anthropology, this concept was a useful way of thinking about rites of passage. Many societies have rites of passage: Think of graduation ceremonies, confirmation ceremonies in churches and synagogues, and membership ceremonies for social and professional organizations. The rite of passage is the in-between stage as the individual passes from one state to another.

A study of adults making the transition to living with chronic kidney disease identified points where liminality occurred (Molzahn et al., 2008). For our purposes, three transitions the authors identified are relevant. The first was normal to not normal. People with kidney disease talked about trying to live a normal life while making changes that were not normal to them. The second transition was worse off to better off. Patients experienced better overall health with treatments that made them evaluate themselves as better off, but their treatments were long and painful and made them feel they were worse off. The third transition was alone to connected. Patients talked about "putting on a brave face" for friends and family but really feeling alone. Yet they also made new friends who were fellow patients, and that was an unexpected benefit.

These three transitions—normal–not normal, worse off–better off, and alone–connected—apply to you, as well. Reading this book is part of a transition journey from where you are now to where you will be later. As you begin to change, you experience the normal–not normal liminality. Sometimes a normal that is bad feels better than an unknown. The same duality is true for worse off–better off. As you begin to have a life energized more by your strengths than characterized by your weaknesses, you will sometimes feel better off and sometimes worse off. You will also have times of being alone and times of being connected.

Why, then, would liminality be a good thing? What advantages are there to being "in between"? One advantage is that being in between leaves room for things that do not fit cleanly in the either–or: Liminality is the complexity of both–and. A second advantage is that embracing liminality is how you journey to your goals. Being "on the path" is by definition a time of liminality. If you resist it, you will not stay long enough on your journey but instead will try to prematurely close it off or turn around to go back. But learning to stay on the path forward is the way to continue to progress toward your recovery goals.

RECOVERY IS THE IN-BETWEEN TIME

I hope you agree that your recovery will be different than just not having problems you now have. Rather, recovery is creating a new and complex self that is active in your life. If you see recovery as a time of in between, you will be able to better tolerate the challenges.

Here is a quote from Andre Malraux, a French writer, explorer, and diplomat, to a friend on the occasion of reading the proofs of the friend's upcoming autobiography: "You did not come back from hell with empty hands." You, the reader of this book, did not come forward from your childhood with empty hands. You have strengths and capabilities and competencies that will sustain your journey.

RESOURCES

Digital Resources

For many survivors, "recovery" is a term associated with recovery from substance abuse. There are physical and online communities in addition to traditional 12-step programs that can help you recover from substance abuse.

- The website The Temper provides a list of 24 in-person and online sober communities (https://www.thetemper.com/sober-communities-beyond-traditional-aa).
- Rethink Mental Illness is a comprehensive website with information, further reading, contacts, and plans for people seeking recovery from mental illness (https://www.rethink.org/advice-and-information/living-with-mental-illness/treatment-and-support/recovery).
- The St. Louis Empowerment Center has a webpage dedicated to the five stages of recovery, describing the characteristics, dangers, and role of professional or peer support at each stage (https://www.dbsaempowerment.org/programs-and-services/specific-program-information/five-stages-recovery-process).

Print Resources

- *201 Positive Psychology Applications: Promoting Well-Being in Individuals and Communities*, by Fredrike Bannink (Norton,

2017). Although directed at counselors for use with clients, this user-friendly book contains exercises to promote well-being in emotions, relationships, meaning, engagement, and accomplishments.

- *8 Keys to Safe Trauma Recovery: Take-Charge Strategies to Empower Your Healing,* by Babette Rothschild (Norton, 2010). This book presents eight keys to recovery that are specific paths to healing. For example, one key is "remembering is not required," and another is "reconcile forgiveness and shame." Much of the content explains the keys and shows how they apply to people's stories.
- *The Posttraumatic Growth Workbook: Coming Through Trauma Wiser, Stronger, and More Resilient,* by Richard Tedeschi and Bret Moore (New Harbinger, 2016). This workbook presents information on posttraumatic growth and provides exercises to help you find meaning, identify your strengths, and build connections. Although the workbook is directed toward trauma survivors in general, the content is helpful for sexual abuse survivors.

CHAPTER 4

RESILIENCE

Recovery Milestones

This chapter will help you:

1. **comprehend** how resilience protects against adversity,
2. **appreciate** how resilience helps recovery after trauma, and
3. **identify** your own sources of resilience.

Has this experience happened to you? You are talking with a friend, and you describe some of the abuse you experienced as a child. And this person says to you, "But you are so strong!" That has happened to me over and over. I would be talking about my abuse and its aftermath, even minimally, and friends would tell me how strong I was. And I heard that, too, after I experienced major disruptions at my place of work, and after my husband left me and our 40-year marriage. "But Betsy, you are so strong." And I would want to say to that person, "You have no idea what you are talking about. *I am not strong!*" And I wondered what they saw that I did not. Now, I know that *resilience* is that "strong" thing, and that we do, indeed, have it. And even better, we can make more of it.

Average adults experience a range of potentially traumatic events and exhibit a variety of reactions to those events. Not every person who experiences a particular traumatic event, such as a natural disaster (like flooding or a hurricane), responds in the same way. In addition to differences among people in their reactions to the same event, there are differences within one person to the same type of event repeated over time, such as the death of someone they know. All these differences are what we call "variability," and there are two kinds of variability in people's responses to trauma. The first is interindividual variability: There are differences among people in their responses to the same traumatic event. The second is intraindividual variability: There are differences within one person in their responses to repeated traumatic events.

What explains these differences? Historically, psychologists began to think about this question when they were helping children after World War II. During the war, children were exposed to or knew of bombings, loss of food and shelter, deaths, and other combat horrors. Psychologists expected that children would show significant problems after the war, including anxiety and a terrible fear of being abandoned or left behind. What psychologists found was that the children who had stayed with their parents during the war were not as traumatized as the children sent to live in the country, where it was safer. Psychologists speculated that being with their parents, even during combat, was less stressful than being separated from their parents, even when they experienced no combat trauma during the separation.

More recently, the U.S. terrorist attacks of September 11, 2001 (known as "9/11") propelled a dramatic increase in research on variable responses to trauma. In the 20 years before 2000, 780 studies were published on psychological responses to disaster; in the 20 years after, 3,500 articles were published. In research on the aftermath of 9/11, psychologists found high levels of posttraumatic stress and no posttraumatic stress, and every level in between, among adults who personally experienced 9/11. In a parallel fashion, psychologists found stress levels ranging from high to nonexistent among adults who witnessed the devastation only on television or social media or who read about it in news accounts. What can explain this variable response to trauma? This chapter describes one explanation: the effects of resilience.

WHAT IS RESILIENCE?

The most influential study of resilience began in 1955, when all babies born on the Hawaiian island of Kauai were enrolled (Werner, 1993). The participants are still being followed; the latest series of interviews occurred when they were in their 40s (McCubbin, 2016). The Kauai study researchers initially divided the children into groups based on what was seen at the time as "risk"—factors believed to create life difficulties. One group of children was defined as *high risk:* They grew up in poverty and experienced stress or conflict in their families (e.g., a parent with mental illness or alcoholism, family violence). During elementary school, most of the high-risk children had learning problems. By age 18, many had unwanted pregnancies or criminal records.

But as they were followed over time, some of these high-risk children became successful adults. When interviewed in their 30s to see how their lives had progressed, these successful high-risk children were now stable in their marital and family lives, were succeeding in jobs and careers, and reported high life satisfaction. What accounted for the differences between their lives and the lives of the high-risk children who continued to have major life difficulties into adulthood? The researchers identified four reasons. One was that the successful children had a "temperament," or personality, during childhood and adolescence that allowed them to make friends easily. The second reason was that they developed skills as they grew up that translated into success as an adult—for example, success in their jobs. The third reason was that they believed in themselves. And the fourth reason was they had social resources—people who believed in them and became trusted parent substitutes and companions in their lives. These social resources included grandparents, authority figures such as teachers, church group leaders, and neighbors.

The Kauai study helped psychologists define *resilience* as "positive adaptation during or following significant adversity or risk" (Masten et al., 2009, p. 118). One of the Kauai study researchers said that the stories of these resilient people showed the "healing powers of hope in individual lives" (Werner, 1993, p. 514). The idea behind this view of resilience is that it shows up when people are experiencing adversity.

The concept of resilience includes two related terms. One is *risk*. In the study of Kauai children, "risk" was defined by what psychologists knew at the time to be things that usually led to negative outcomes later in life. Adverse childhood experiences (ACEs), discussed in Chapter 2, are a risk we have learned more about in the past decade. "Cumulative risk" is having several risk factors at the same time or having risk factors that accumulate over time.

The second term related to resilience is *protective factors*, which are things that have been demonstrated through research to be associated with positive outcomes in people with high levels of risk. In the Kauai study, for example, a protective factor was a strong relationship with a person who was trustworthy and dependable and became a parent substitute. Protective factors can be qualities within the child, within the family, or within the community that surrounds the growing child.

After these early findings, psychologists completed more research to identify protective factors that could be deliberately increased so that children would have better outcomes even if they were exposed to adversity. Masten and colleagues (2009) identified sets of protective factors. One set exists within people and includes a sense of meaning in life, skills and attitudes that help solve problems, and self-esteem. Another set of protective factors are in the social context, such as parent involvement in the child's education, low levels of conflict in the family, and connections between the child and other children who are rule abiding.

It might help you now to think back to your childhood. What protective factors can you identify? For me, the woman who lived next door was a mother substitute. She fixed me lunches, spent time with me, and even disciplined me when I helped her daughter open all the hidden Christmas presents ahead of time! Did you have a neighbor or a teacher or a grandparent like that? Were there other protective factors in yourself or your family or your community?

Another approach to understanding resilience is to study many people, some of whom are at risk, at one point in time and to compare those who have resilience resources to those do not. A study of 1,000 older adults used this approach to identify resilience factors that led to healthy aging in the face of challenges (Jeste et al., 2013). The challenges these older adults faced were difficulties in physical health (e.g., pain, poor health, limitations in activity because of illness), lowered cognitive functioning (e.g., attention difficulties, poor memory), and problems in mental health (e.g., depression).

The researchers found that successful aging—positive responses to challenges over time—was related to three protective factors they called "hardiness," "persistence," and "optimism." *Hardiness* is being able to manage life changes, including those caused by illness and unexpected events; feeling a sense of control over events; and viewing change as a good thing. *Persistence* is continuing to give one's best efforts to achieve goals even in the face of obstacles and roadblocks. *Optimism* is believing in oneself as capable of achieving what one attempts, including learning from mistakes. These are protective factors; they operate in the middle of adversity. They increase our resilience as we face adversity.

"Broaden and build theory" was developed by Barbara Fredrickson (2001), a psychologist who has studied positive emotions as another protective factor in adversity. In her model, the first step is "broaden." We broaden by using positive emotions to expand (broaden) the number of response options available to us during adversity. As an example, recall that one response to stress is flight. That response reduces our options quickly to only one action—"run away." We are more likely to overcome adversity if we expand our response options. Fredrickson argued that positive emotions, such as interest or pride, can help us broaden our view of possible response options.

The second step is "build." What we are building are resources—the physical, intellectual, emotional, spiritual, and social practices we use during adversity. As we build our resources and experience success dealing with adversity, we are motivated to broaden and further expand our response options. Then we build more resources, further expand our response options, and so on. The visual representation of the broaden and build model is a spiral, in which we move upward, away from adversity and toward increasing amounts of positive emotions. The positive emotions widen the range of actions we then identify and try out.

How might that spiral look in practice? For me, my go-to method of dealing with any strong emotion was "intellectualizing": I immediately wondered, "Why am I feeling this way?" and then spent my time and energy thinking about events, rather than feeling the emotions. The result of that process, over and over, was that I feared and avoided having emotions. Broadening happened when I started approaching emotions with curiosity and confidence, simply feeling the emotion as being present rather than distancing myself from the emotion by thinking about it.

The positive emotions involved in repeated cycles of broaden and build have important roles. First, they serve as "antidotes" to negative emotions, what Fredrickson (2001) called the "undoing hypothesis." Positive emotions help us place the negative events in our lives in a larger context, which can lessen or undo the events' emotional impact on us. Second, positive emotions fuel resilience; they help us bounce back from adversity more quickly. Third, the spiral of improvement corrects the spiral of depression, which is downward and narrowing. So positive emotions are more important than simply making us "feel good"; rather, they improve our physical health and psychological resilience.

So how does resilience work? Psychologists have focused on four mechanisms. First, resilience is a developmental process. Recall the Kauai study, in which resilience was measured over time as at-risk children took different paths. Second, resilience works through ways that help buffer adversity. An example is attachment; having a supportive adult in their life helps at-risk children create a strong attachment bond that is not available from their parents. Third, resilience is an educational process; it is composed partly of skills that can be learned so people can use them when they face adversity. Finally, resilience involves biological processes: Adversity affects the brain and body systems in negative ways, and resilience reduces that negative impact through biological pathways.

One of the most important aspects of resilience is self-acceptance. Self-acceptance is related to well-being and is part of hardiness and optimism. Insights From Psychology 4.1 describes a study of male survivors of childhood sexual abuse thinking about self-acceptance.

To summarize, here is what we know about resilience:

- It is composed of resources—protective factors—within and outside the person that protect them from the effects of adversity.
- It has a critical role in helping the person manage ongoing adversity.
- The parts of resilience are hardiness, persistence, and optimism.

Insights From Psychology 4.1

Self-Acceptance Among Male Survivors of Childhood Sexual Abuse

There is more research with women who are survivors of childhood sexual abuse than with men. That may be because researchers who study this subject are often women who wish to better understand the experiences of other women. It may also be that society, including psychologists, struggle to acknowledge male victims because the experience of childhood sexual abuse stands in contrast to traditional notions of masculinity, namely, power and control. Those assumptions of masculinity reflect certain values about what is involved in "being a man." Researchers interviewed 16 resilient male survivors regarding the effects of their abuse on their values of masculinity (Kia-Keating et al., 2005). In this study, all the survivors experienced contact abuse (oral, anal, or genital intercourse) from perpetrators who were fathers, siblings, mothers, male relatives, and family friends.

The authors first described traditional masculine values related to self-acceptance in three areas. First, aggression and power, especially physical aggression, are valued and expected. Second, values seen as traditionally feminine, especially emotions such as tenderness or compassion, are avoided. Third, there is an expectation of toughness, confidence, and self-reliance. The goal of the study was to understand how the male survivors of childhood sexual abuse accepted themselves within the framework of these masculine values.

The interviews demonstrated that all the men had difficulty accepting themselves within the values of conventional masculinity, namely toughness, physical strength, and stoicism. The participants saw their abuse history as contradicting the values of conventional masculinity. They found self-acceptance as they replaced those traditional masculine values with other values. For example, the value of physical toughness was replaced with valuing alternatives to violence and ending the cycle of abuse by not becoming a perpetrator. The value of stoicism, mental toughness, and "not feeling" was replaced with the value of relating and compassion.

- Resilience may be strengthened through the broaden and build model, in which positive emotions create flexibility and creativity in response to adversity and then an upward spiral of improved coping.

Resilience After Interpersonal Trauma

Adversity is a common human experience, and resilience plays a protective role in response to adversity in general, but the focus in this book is on a particular type of adversity—childhood sexual abuse—that is interpersonal in nature and deeply traumatic, occurs at a time in the individual's development when they are most vulnerable, and is likely to result in later impairments in physical and emotional functioning. Fortunately, research indicates that resilience also plays a protective role for people who have experienced interpersonal trauma.

Resilience has been shown to help survivors of abuse cope with the damage in their lives. As a reminder, or if you have not read Chapter 2, some of the types of damage seen in adults who experienced childhood sexual abuse are self-blame, depression, loss of hope, posttraumatic stress symptoms, physical illness symptoms, and feelings of loss of control. A group of psychologists studied 200 young women who had experienced childhood sexual abuse and examined the effects of resilience on their emotions and quality of life. The women who had higher resilience had lower depression and better quality of life. Thus, resilience helped these women live better lives even after an interpersonal trauma such as childhood sexual abuse.

In addition, research has identified the same component parts of resilience in adults after childhood sexual abuse as in adults who experience adversity outside the realm of childhood sexual abuse. Researchers analyzed the results of published studies about resilience among adults after childhood sexual abuse and drew two conclusions (Marriott et al., 2014). First, they noted that inner resources such as self-esteem, hardiness, and mastery ("mastery" is being successful in coping) increased resilience. Second, supportive factors outside the individual, such as having a caring person who was a parent surrogate and being part of a religious group, increased resilience.

Self-Assessment 4.1 is a scale for measuring resilience that lists the many ways resilience can be exhibited. Identifying how much you agree with each statement will help you better understand your current level of resilience and areas for which you might set goals. Bear in mind that your score reflects your view of your resilience at this point in time; this book will show you strategies for building your resilience, and your score will increase during the course of your journey toward recovery.

So how can you put what we've learned about resilience into action in your own recovery journey? The sections that follow show how resilience can be a part of your life.

Resilience Is How You Think

Resilience has a lot to do with how we think about situations. We show resilience when we adopt a thinking style that makes problem solving easier; Self-Assessment 4.2 helps you explore your thinking styles. We show resilience when we show "hardiness": the belief that we can approach barriers, figure out how to get through them or around them, and make those changes confidently. We show resilience when we believe we can influence our surroundings, from our personal environment (for example, who we choose as friends) to our physical environment. Lastly, we show resilience when we're optimistic: when we believe that we are capable of learning from

Self-Assessment 4.1

Measuring Your Resilience

Directions: In your journal or note-taking app, write the number that best reflects your agreement or disagreement with each of the items below. A 1 indicates your strongest disagreement, and a 7 indicates your strongest agreement; you can also use any number between 1 and 7.

1. I usually manage one way or another.
2. I feel proud that I have accomplished things in life.
3. I usually take things in stride.
4. I am friends with myself.
5. I feel that I can handle many things at a time.
6. I am determined.
7. I can get through difficult times because I've had trouble before.
8. I have self-discipline.
9. I keep interested in things.
10. I can usually find something to laugh about.
11. My belief in myself gets me through hard times.
12. In an emergency, I'm someone people can generally rely on.
13. My life has meaning.
14. When I'm in a difficult situation, I can usually find my way out of it.

Calculate your score by adding up the numbers you wrote for the 14 items. You can also calculate separate scores for the items as reflecting the way you are (2, 4, 6, 8, 9, 11, and 13) and what you do (1, 3, 5, 7, 10, 12, and 14). You might also consider the balance between the score that reflects "the way you are" and the score that reflects "what you do"—are they about the same, or is one score higher than the other? In your journal or note-taking app, describe how you see yourself as more one than the other, or how you are balanced between them. Can you set a goal for increasing your resilience score?

Self-Assessment 4.2

What Is Your Thinking Style?

One aspect of resilience is being able to solve problems. That may sound simple, but it is not. Good problem solving is hijacked in many ways: by too much emotion to be able to step back from the problem, by rigid thinking styles that get in our way, by too much concern over how others view us.

The skill we are interested in for this self-assessment is *explanatory styles of thinking*: This is a long term that means how we think about the things that happen to us in our lives. Take a minute and think of a problem that is occurring in your life right now. Say it out loud to yourself, and if you want, write it down in your journal or note-taking app. Now answer these three questions about the problem: Who caused the problem? How long will the problem last? How much of my life is affected by this problem? Write down those answers. Now reconsider your answers to the three questions, simplifying them to one of only two response options.

The first question—Who caused the problem?—addresses the thinking style of "personalization," and the answer choices are "me" or "not me." The second question—How long will the problem last?—addresses the thinking style of "permanence," and the answer choices are "always" or "not always." The third question—How much of my life is affected by this problem?—addresses the thinking style of "pervasiveness," and the answer choices are "everything" or "not everything."

Let's look at the example of a survivor who asked a friend out for coffee but the friend declined, saying she had to spend time with her spouse. The survivor's thinking style might be as follows:

> Who caused the problem? Me. No one cares about me. How long will the problem last? Always. I never will be able to have friends. How much of my life is affected by this problem? Everything. I am rejected by this friend, and when I am rejected, I am depressed and cut myself.

This thinking style makes problem solving almost impossible because the survivor jumped to inaccurate conclusions that took them away from a good analysis of the problem.

Self-Assessment 4.2 (*Continued*)

A better way of thinking is to develop "not me, not always, not everything" responses. The survivor might think,

> I would have liked to go out for coffee with her, but she had a conflict [*not me*]. I know her husband works long hours, and it makes sense that he wants to spend time with her. I will ask her again next week [*not always*]. Meanwhile, I will go watch that series I have heard about [*not everything*].

This better way is how we correct the following "thinking traps":

- *Personalizing:* We believe we are responsible for problems or situations that we are not actually responsible for.
- *Externalizing:* We blame others for problems or situations that they are not responsible for.
- *Mind reading:* We assume we know what other people are thinking without asking them directly.
- *Overgeneralizing:* We make a firm judgment without having enough evidence about another person, an event, or a group of people.
- *Catastrophizing:* We assume something will be as bad as it could possibly be.

our mistakes as well as our successes and that we can get better at making healthy choices over time.

Resilience Is How You Feel

For most survivors, emotions are challenging. We deny certain feelings, we feel hijacked by feelings, we are confused about our feelings and cannot differentiate them from one another. It is so important to know that being resilient does not mean having only positive feelings. Much of the emotional part of resilience means being able to experience a negative feeling, to not be overwhelmed by it, and to allow ourselves to learn from it. Resilience also includes the experience of self-esteem—of valuing the self.

The importance of meaning is one of the themes found throughout research on resilience. (I discuss meaning in more depth in Chapter 6.) Briefly, we experience meaning in life when events in our life seem to be related to our goals, or to future events, or to hoped-for consequences. Meaning is also the experience of mattering, to someone else or in general. Meaning is continuity, a big banner that connects various events in our life. And meaning is coherence: Things make sense. When we focus on and rebuild meaning, our life can become a newly discovered element in a different story. Meaning is important in resilience because it promotes engagement in life.

Resilience Is What You Do

We show resilience in the actions we take. *Resilience* can be thought of as the development of competence despite severe adversity (Luthar et al., 2000). *Competence* is our ability to do what we do well. Self-Assessment 4.1 gave you information on your resilience. Attitudes, beliefs, thoughts, and feelings are all very important. But to be resilient, we need to put those attitudes, beliefs, thoughts, and feelings to work making changes in our lives.

LEARNING ABOUT RESILIENCE FROM A SPECIAL GROUP OF ADULTS

We can learn about resilience from an unusual group—people who know ahead of time that they will be stressed beyond their capacity. A recent research project conducted by six scientists of human performance studied 122 candidates for the Special Forces as they completed a 3-week selection course (Gucciardi et al., 2021). The selection course involved multiple tasks that built in challenges (for example, unrealistic time expectations) during physical and mental fatigue. The researchers were interested in *perseverance*, which they defined as sustained pursuit of a goal when there are many barriers to reaching that goal. Defined this way, perseverance is a key part of resilience following the complex trauma of childhood sexual abuse.

The candidates answered questions to measure their perseverance by rating how much they agreed with a series of statements (for example, "I strive for continued success"). The outcome measure was success in being chosen for further training; only 26 of the 122 candidates succeeded. The results of this study showed that perseverance predicted the candidates' success in selection better than their age (which was related to success in physical tasks) and their amount of preparation.

What does this study tell us? First, perseverance is more than one single action; it is multiple, sustained actions directed toward valued goals, and it represents the importance of purpose and flexibility. Second, perseverance is not simply having a desire to learn a new skill; rather, perseverance continues under challenging conditions, which are part of its definition. Third, perseverance is more than physical and mental prowess. All 122 candidates were fully physically and mentally prepared for the rigors of the course. I think if we could hear from the people who succeeded in those very difficult conditions (adversity), they would tell us that everyone, including you and I, has the potential for perseverance and that we can increase our resilience in the face of great adversity by focusing on our own hardiness, persistence, and optimism.

RESOURCES

Digital Resources

- The PositivePsychology.com website contains resources to help teachers, counselors, and others increase resilience in their students and clients. It is user friendly and provides content and exercises you can download (https://positivepsychology. com/category/resilience).

- The Substance Abuse and Mental Health Services Administration, known as SAMHSA, is a federal agency within the U.S. Department of Health and Human Services. Its website contains resources about resilience and stress management organized by topic and by audience (https://www.samhsa.gov/ dbhis-collections/resilience-stress-management).

Print Resources

- *Resilience: Hard-Won Wisdom for Living a Better Life*, by Eric Greitens (First Mariner Books, 2015). For some of us, stories from other survivors have helped greatly. This book is a series of letters from a Navy SEAL to a comrade who struggled with posttraumatic stress disorder after returning home from combat duty and coped through avoidance, including substance abuse. The author drew from his own experience and from the ideas of both ancient and modern philosophers to talk about experiencing pain, practicing self-compassion, creating happiness, and more.
- *The Mindful Self-Compassion Workbook: A Proven Way to Accept Yourself, Build Inner Strength, and Thrive*, by Kristin Neff (Guilford Press, 2018). One important part of building resilience is increasing our self-compassion so that we are freed up to face adversity. This workbook contains many exercises for learning about self-compassion and its role in improving interpersonal relationships and dealing with shame.
- *The Resilience Factor: 7 Keys to Finding Your Inner Strength and Overcoming Life's Hurdles*, by Karen Reivich and Andrew Shatte (Broadway Books, 2002). This practical book teaches

seven competencies that build resilience, some of which were introduced in this chapter. Although the book is not directed to trauma survivors, the content is applicable. The seven competencies are emotional regulation, impulse control, analysis of problems, empathy, optimism, perseverance, and connection.

- *The Resilience Workbook: Essential Skills to Recover From Stress, Trauma, and Adversity*, by Glenn Schiraldi (New Harbinger, 2017). As the title suggests, this workbook teaches specific skills for managing distressing emotions and building inner strength. Examples of these skills are expressive writing, meaning and purpose, and active coping. There are many exercises and self-assessments.

CHAPTER 5

GRIEF

Recovery Milestones

This chapter will help you

1. **understand** the concept of grief accurately,
2. **realize** how and why grief is present after childhood sexual abuse, and
3. **identify** how grieving will be a part of your recovery.

I wrote poems while I was in early stages of my recovery. I had never written poetry before, and never did again. I don't know enough about poetry to understand what makes a poem "high quality," and that was a good thing because I did not self-censor. In those poems, I returned often to a few pictures I had in my head of what had happened to me. One was a river with bodies floating in it. One was a landscape with rocks and cliffs and shards of glass against a blood red sky. And one was a little girl, frozen in the snow, her tears ice on her face, with wolves keeping her company. That picture remains vivid to me still, and I realize that it was a picture of my grief.

Why am I asking you to read about grief? It may seem that the other chapter topics are "positive," and they are. But a big part of your recovery is grieving what you have lost. There are some similarities between childhood sexual abuse and bereavement (Fleming &

Belanger, 2001). First, they are both events that happened in the past and cannot be changed. No amount of re-imaging will bring back a lost loved one, and no amount of re-imaging will give you your lost childhood back. Second, others may overlook these events or even shun you because of them. Some grievers find their experience to be "disenfranchised," or not deemed legitimate; this is often true for abuse survivors, as well. Friends or family may find it hard to accept and allow your grief. My goal in this chapter is to help you accept grief as part of your recovery.

WHAT IS GRIEF?

For an experience that is virtually universal, grief is still difficult for psychologists and others to understand accurately. We know that the death of someone close to us is considered a major life stressor. For example, the Holmes–Rahe Life Stress Inventory has bereavement as three of its top 20 life events causing stress—death of a spouse, death of a family member, and death of a close friend (Holmes & Rahe, 1967). We know that, as with trauma, there are many differences among people in how they experience and express grief. Most important for our purposes is that although grief seems to coexist with pain, psychologists are beginning to recognize a positive role for grief in response to adversity and loss.

Scientific interest in grief was initiated by two psychiatrists whose clinical work with patients led them to think about grief in new ways. One of these was Erich Lindemann, a psychiatrist at Harvard, who practiced at Massachusetts General Hospital in the 1940s. He counseled patients after limb amputations and noticed that their psychological reactions after their surgeries most resembled a set of responses he would label as grief. Then, on a November evening in 1942, with hundreds of people packed into the Cocoanut Grove nightclub, a fire spread quickly and devastated the building.

More than 400 people were killed, and many more were brought to the hospital where Lindemann practiced. Surgeons successfully treated the burn injuries, but their patients remained despairing. Lindemann realized that their responses of anger, depression, hallucinations, and the like were symptoms of deep loss that were very like what he had observed in his amputation patients. He wrote an influential paper (Lindemann, 1944) defining grief as a psychosocial problem rather than a psychiatric problem, and thus a normal life experience.

The second psychiatrist, Elisabeth Kübler-Ross, focused on grief reactions, this time with patients who were dying of a terminal illness. She described what she saw as stages in how her patients came to terms with their own death (Kübler-Ross, 1969). Those stages are *denial*, when the person refuses to believe the diagnosis; *anger*, when the person lashes out at people close to him or her; *bargaining*, when the person tries to negotiate with fate or a personal God for a change in circumstances; *depression*, when the person despairs over their coming death; and *acceptance*, when the person embraces their mortality.

Grief expresses itself in distinguishable areas. Emotional expressions of grieving include sadness, despair, anxiety, guilt, numbness, pain, and loneliness, among other emotions. Cognitive (thought) expressions of grief include feeling shocked, being distracted, ruminating over the loss, and searching for meaning. Physical expressions include sleep disturbances, tightness of the chest, increased vulnerability to disease because of a compromised immune system, and nervous tension. Spiritual expressions are a withdrawal from a faith community, a lack of hope, and anger toward a deity.

A "model" of grief is a picture of how it works and what its parts are. Contemporary models of grief have been validated through research that can help us understand grief after childhood sexual abuse. I'll discuss two of these models: the dual process model and meaning reconstruction.

Dual Process Model of Grief

The dual process model proposes that people who are grieving engage in two "processes," or courses of action. The first process is "loss oriented," when the person is focused on the loss. Within the loss orientation, for example, the person struggles to accept the reality of their loss and experiences the pain of grief (mourning). Within the second process, "restoration orientation," the person makes a new life after the loss by taking time away from the pain of grief and developing new roles and identities. The critical part of the dual process model is "oscillation": The grieving person changes back and forth between loss and restoration, many times, and over time. The developers of the dual process model, Stroebe and Schut (1999; see Fiore, 2019, for a review of related studies), believed it is healthy for the grieving person to experience grief as a back-and-forth change between pain and reengagement in life. Thus, this model differs from the perspective that sees grief as a series of tasks or that defines successful grieving as a single event of "moving on."

Meaning Reconstruction in Grief

Meaning reconstruction is a model of grief that focuses on how grievers make sense of their loss by redefining themselves and how they will engage in the world (Neimeyer, 1998). According to this model, people anticipate and understand events in their lives through their own construction of assumptions about the world. A loss or bereavement challenges those assumptions and creates the need to regain an understanding of the world—that is, to reconstruct a sense of meaning. For example, a parent who assumes the world is a just place is shattered by the death of a child through violence. The life story of that parent now is missing the child, who was to have grown up and become an adult companion through life. The parent will need to construct a new meaning of the loss and of their life without the child.

In summary, the experience of grief is being understood with new assumptions about its nature and its purpose. Those new assumptions are as follows:

- Grief used to be seen as having a universal, predictable trajectory; now, grief is seen more as having individual and complex patterns.
- The idea of grief as focused solely on emotions is changing toward an emphasis on the role of beliefs, world assumptions, meaning, and personal identity in addition to emotions.
- The possibility of posttraumatic growth during the grieving process is now better appreciated.

Grief After Childhood Sexual Abuse

As authors Ellen Bass and Laura Davis (2008) noted in their book for survivors of childhood sexual abuse, you and other survivors of childhood sexual abuse have a lot to grieve. You have losses in your past, you experience losses in the present, and you anticipate losses in the future. You probably have losses that you have not even labeled as a loss. You must grieve the death of a worldview in which children are loved and cared for, it is safe to trust, and childhood innocence is precious. You may have held on to a fantasy that your childhood was happy or perfect. I know that I did. Giving up that illusion means grieving its loss. Your abuse may have made relationships in your family difficult or nonexistent. That is a loss as well.

Sofka (1999) outlined a framework for identifying losses after childhood sexual abuse that divides those losses into two main categories: (a) losses of a physical, emotional, and psychological nature and (b) losses of a social nature (that is, involving others). Within the physical–emotional–psychological category are the loss of virginity and sexual purity, the loss of control, the loss of self-esteem, damage to a sense of safety and security, and damages in mental health. Within the social category are losses related to betrayal, family estrangement, difficulty in initiating and maintaining relationships, and stigma.

It is worth noting that family estrangement is a significant loss for survivors. Survivors face the challenge of losing their connection to their families after disclosing their abuse. This outcome often occurs if the abuse was in the family. Family members inevitably take sides, and some even demand the expulsion of the survivor from the family unit. But this outcome can occur even if the perpetrator was outside the family, for blame is still placed on the family for allowing the abuse to happen.

Research on the reactions of "nonoffending guardians"—that is, parents and other support figures, such as grandparents, who were not the perpetrators of abuse—shows a high level of ambivalence after the disclosure of abuse (see Bolen & Lamb, 2004). For example, the guardian may have a close relationship with the perpetrator but also wants to protect the child. Or the guardian may feel forced to choose which to believe, the child or the perpetrator. This ambivalence leads to contradictory behaviors. For example, the guardian might vacillate between having the perpetrator continue living in the home or having a close relationship with the family versus having the perpetrator rejected from the family unit.

There has been little scholarly research on the topic of grief among survivors. One study that can help us understand the losses associated with childhood sexual abuse analyzed interviews with 52 survivors (Bourdon & Cook, 1994). The participants were all women ages 26 to 35. Half had been sexually abused before age 5 and another 30% before age 8. Only 13% of the participants were abused by strangers; the others experienced incest by fathers, siblings, or other relatives. The most important finding of this study was the large number of losses that the participants rated as "completely true for me." Some were losses of childhood, such as a loss of innocence and of the feeling that "I had a childhood." Others were personal losses—of a sense of identity, self-respect, positive body image, and the ability to have feelings. Still others were losses of connection to others, including the ability to trust, experience being cared for, and know that one is supported by others. Some losses were related to sexuality, such as feeling sexually pure and feeling entitled to sexual pleasure. Lastly, some were future losses, including of dreams for the future.

A more recent study of 116 female college-age survivors expanded on these findings (Murthi & Espelage, 2005). Half of this group experienced contact abuse and the other half noncontact forms of abuse. These young women endorsed losses in three categories. The first was a loss of optimism; examples were losing the ability to feel interest in life and losing a sense of meaning. The second category was a loss of self—feeling like something within oneself had died. The third was a loss of childhood, such as losing innocence and growing up "too fast."

One specific loss experienced by survivors of childhood sexual abuse is the thought that somehow, they were responsible for the abuse, either by actions in which they engaged or actions which were not carried out. Psychologists call these counterfactual thoughts because these "if only" or "what if" thoughts take the form of mentally replaying the situation and changing the outcome. Adult survivors may think about their past with counterfactual thoughts that explain, justify, or excuse their abuse or that judge their own actions. Research has shown that counterfactual thoughts can lead to depression and anxiety, likely through rumination over how things might have turned out differently or better (see Byrne, 2016). An example of a counterfactual thought is, "I should have told someone about his actions; they would have stopped him. So I am responsible." The person with this thought assumes, without any evidence, that their action would have resulted in a different outcome and that therefore that they were responsible for the abuse, which is not reasonable. These counterfactual thoughts can interfere with the acceptance of grief over the past.

In summary, grief is a very relevant construct for the experience of survivors of childhood sexual abuse. This is true for several reasons:

- The abuse resulted in many losses, including losses of a physical, psychological, and emotional nature and losses of a social nature.
- One particular loss, that of family relationships, applies to many survivors. Disclosing the abuse creates significant tension within the family and often results in loss of connection to the family.
- Survivors sometimes engage in counterfactual thoughts, assuming without evidence that they were responsible for the abuse or for the broken relationships that followed.

HOW DO YOU GRIEVE?

What is the trajectory of grief? What pathway or pattern does it take? I noted previously that it is not usually a smooth path consisting of several stages with essential tasks. And it certainly is not a one-step process. How can we understand grief? Stephen Fleming and Shari Belanger (2001) proposed that there are grieving styles. If we think about grief at its most essential, the griever moves from loss, to pain, to acceptance. That is a simplified description; it does not imply that we make one "stop" at each stage; rather, we are likely to cycle back and forth between stops, as described in the dual process model. Each of those stops is important. In loss, we lose what we have. That is clear in bereavement, but it is also clear in the aftermath of childhood sexual abuse. In pain, we suffer from the absence of the loved one (bereavement) or the many wounds of abuse. In acceptance, we become a new person, one who has resolved the loss, maintains bonds with the lost one through remembrance or honoring (if the loss is bereavement), and finds new meaning.

Fleming and Belanger (2001) described three styles that differ in their progression through the "stops" (loss, pain, and acceptance): typical grieving, chronic grieving, and delayed grief. In typical grieving, the person moves through the stops eventually, even if they cycle back and forth among them, to achieve acceptance and growth. In chronic grieving, the person stops at pain, constantly reliving the victimization and hurt. In delayed grief, the person refuses to experience the pain stop, instead detouring into avoidance and stagnation. As Fleming and Belanger described it,

> Victims, in working through the pain, reassess the nature of the past relationship with the perpetrator and its impact. In understanding what has been lost and accepting this reality . . . they are able to take control of the past, which involves directing the blame and anger appropriately at the perpetrator, thus releasing the guilt and internal anger. (p. 323)

What are we doing while we are moving through the stops? Cacciatore (2012) proposed a model of grieving named the Selah model. *Selah* is a Hebrew word meaning to pause, to mull over, to "sit with." Cacciatore's model explains grieving as a focus on the self and a focus on others. When the self is the focus, the goal is *attunement*; "to attune" means to bring into harmony. During the focus on self, the person engages in the activity of being with grief and bringing the self into harmony with grief. Simply sitting with grief is challenging, painful, and even frightening. That may be because it requires solitude, self-awareness, and self-compassion. But being with grief is also possible through storytelling, journaling, meditation, prayer, being outside in nature, and creative activities such as poetry and art.

When others are the focus, the goal is "responsible action." In this focus, you see others' sufferings as one with your own, and you may feel called to a higher purpose by your grief. Meaning making is an important part of this goal, as is appreciation for the new ways in which you understand the world and your place in it. Examples of responsible action are becoming an advocate for persons who have suffered as you have or pursuing a calling to a higher purpose (such as helping others, making the world a better place, giving of your time and money, volunteering).

You may think that the goal of managing emotions during grief is to reduce their intensity and to avoid strong emotions completely. But there is an important role for expressing emotions, even when that process is painful. Longitudinal studies (which follow participants over time) have shown that people living with a diagnosis of cancer or the experience of infertility find that intentionally expressing their emotions is beneficial (see Stanton & Low, 2012, for a review of these studies). When people are asked to engage in "expressive writing"—that is, to write down their thoughts and feelings about the stressor—they report more distress but find the intervention to be helpful. A comprehensive meta-analysis of expressive writing interventions for people experiencing distress evaluated 146 separate studies to determine whether this intervention was effective, and for whom (Frattaroli, 2006). This analysis established that, overall, people in distress experience improved mental and physical health after engaging in expressive writing about their distress.

Why is expressing emotions helpful? It feels quite painful as you do it. But there are several reasons why emotional expression is effective. First, you put a name to your emotional experience: You gain valuable distance from an emotion when you observe it and label it. The name may be a feeling word, but it can also be a picture or a sound. Second, you can see your experience differently when you fill out the details. Third, emotional expression may help you determine how you wish to continue to interact with your grief. Fourth, as you become attuned to your grief through your emotions, you are completing part of the grieving experience. Self-Assessment 5.1 presents a way to attune yourself to your grief.

Companioning Grief

Alan Wolfelt (2006) is a nationally recognized educator, author, and counselor on grief. He has taken the position that grief is not an illness to be treated but an experience to be "companioned" by someone whose role is to honor the grief, to bear witness to it, and to give it a voice, without trying to change the grief or help the person who is grieving. When that happens, there is the possibility of growth through the grief. Here is why that is possible, according to Wolfelt:

- Growth means change. Wolfelt saw grieving as the best way to create change. "Mourning" is not staying in the past, but rather accepting the likelihood that grief will create a new way of interacting with life.
- Growth means encountering pain. Encountering all the pain of all our losses at once would be unbearable. So "grief" means, over time, taking pieces of the loss and embracing those pains. The dual process model applies here; we move from pain (loss) to construction (restoration) to pain again.
- Growth means a new inner balance with no end points. There is no stop sign to growth! You do not reach the end of grieving.

Self-Assessment 5.1

A Grief Diary

This exercise is meant to help you see that the intensity of your grief changes over time. It also introduces you to the idea of being with your grief. For a week, using your journal or note-taking app, select times each day when you are experiencing grief about some aspect of your past. Use the focusing questions below to write more about what you have lost. Then rate your grief on a scale of 1 (*lowest*) to 5 (*highest*).

There are four focusing questions (Kosminsky, 2012):

1. Who or what was lost?
2. What feelings do you have when you think of that loss?
3. Is this loss connected with another loss that came before it?
4. What was that other loss that came before?

Ideally, you will have two or three times each day when you are most attuned to your loss. At the end of the week, write out a summary of what your experience of grief and loss has helped you learn.

Here is how a journal entry might look:

> Early morning. My first waking thought is that I was abused. What was lost was my father to me. The feelings I have are deep, sharp pain and confusion. That loss is connected to losing my good memories of my childhood once I began to confront the reality of my childhood. Losing those memories, realizing they were not accurate, leaves me feeling completely disconnected from my life. I no longer know who I am. This is especially difficult when friends talk about their childhood or I interact with siblings. My grief rating is 4.

But you reach a new inner acceptance of the pain and the reasons for it.

- Growth means exploring our assumptions about life. Recall from Chapter 2 that trauma violates our assumptions about ourselves and the world and our place in it. Those assumptions can be considered, evaluated, and changed.
- Growth means actualizing our losses. How do we "actualize" a loss? Wolfelt argued that rather than dragging us down, a loss frees us up to realize our new potential and gain new resources.

Self-Assessment 5.2 gives you an opportunity to find out how "validating" or "invalidating" you are of your own losses. When you validate your losses, you are a companion for yourself during your grief.

Grief, Loss, and Growth

Recall from Chapter 2 that one dimension of trauma is fear, and that dimension has been studied widely by psychologists and other care providers. Fear is the basis of the posttraumatic stress disorder (PTSD) diagnosis and of most treatments for trauma and PTSD. This chapter has emphasized another dimension of the trauma of childhood sexual abuse, and that is grief. Grief is part of trauma because trauma imposes losses on the person: loss of health, loss of emotional well-being, loss of relationships, loss of safety, loss of the relationship to the perpetrator. Grief is a significant part of the experience of childhood sexual abuse, yet it is rarely acknowledged.

A concept from mindfulness—"radical acceptance"—is an effective way of approaching the work of grieving *Radical acceptance* involves accepting thoughts, feelings, and circumstances instead of avoiding, fighting against, or numbing them. Radical

Self-Assessment 5.2

Do You Invalidate Your Grief?

The purpose of this self-assessment is to shed light on how you talk to yourself about your losses. First, in your journal or note-taking app, write down several losses you experienced because of your childhood sexual abuse. Then write, next to each loss, what you said to yourself when you were able to stand outside of your experience, or what you heard from other people about your experience. Are those statements invalidating or validating?

Invalidating statements communicate the judgment that your reactions are wrong. Here are examples of invalidating statements:

- Time heals everything.
- You are too sensitive.
- It's time you moved on.
- Maybe it was just a misunderstanding.
- Don't play the victim.
- Many other people have had it worse than you.
- God doesn't give you more than you can handle.
- It is all in God's plan.
- Life is just difficult; you are no different from anyone else.

Validating statements communicate self-compassion, which was introduced in Chapter 3. If you did not read that section of the chapter, here is a summary: Self-compassion includes three ways to treat yourself. The first is with kindness; when you are kind to yourself, you give yourself positive support and reduce harsh self-criticism. The second is with connection, or common humanity; this is the recognition that everyone makes mistakes, everyone fails, and it is not an experience to be ashamed of. The third is with mindfulness; you hold negative emotions or thoughts "gently" and do not either become one with them or suppress them.

What might be self-compassionate answers to the invalidating thoughts or words you identified in this assessment? Write those out as well. Here is an example: For the statement "It's time you moved on," a self-compassionate answer would be "No, I need to take all the time I want to. My experience is important, and I will not accept someone else's opinion about it."

acceptance allows you to keep those thoughts, feelings, and experiences present in your attention without any negative judgments. This practice is not the same as thinking the circumstances were good, or even tolerable. It does not mean forgiving your abuser or admitting defeat at their hands. Rather, it is a paradox—something that seems contradictory to fact, and yet is somehow true; when you accept your life as it is, you begin to be able to make changes. It is a realistic assessment of your present that becomes a map for your future.

How can grief have a positive role in your recovery? Grief is the space where you acknowledge your losses, accept them even in their darkness, and see a future. Recall from Chapter 4 that part of resilience is hardiness: being able to manage life changes, feeling a sense of control over events, and viewing change as a good thing. Grief reminds us that some of what we do in recovery is paradoxical: Grief involves mourning, and yet, at the same time, grief involves growth.

Recall the discussion in Chapter 3 of posttraumatic growth. If you have not read that chapter, here is a short summary: Posttraumatic growth is more than a return to "normal" after trauma; it is the creation of enduring, positive growth. That growth often happens in one or more of five areas. The first is changes in how you perceive yourself. An example is seeing yourself as stronger than you thought you were or having a better appreciation for your strengths. The second is changes in your relationships with others. After trauma, we find that we value interpersonal relationships in a new way. The third area is changes in your philosophy of life, such as a new sense of spirituality. The fourth is seeing new possibilities in your life, such as a new job or new interests. The last area of growth is a greater appreciation of life, such as gratitude for the smaller things in life.

Grieving can create a context for growth. This is so because we see ourselves differently after we embrace a role for pain. It is so because grieving helps us consider and change our assumptions about the world. And it is so because of the effort it takes to rebuild our inner worlds.

RESOURCES

Digital Resources

- MastersInCounseling.org is an informational resource that describes more than 100 websites devoted to grief (https://www.MastersInCounseling.org/guide/loss-grief-bereavement). Although many of those websites are focused on bereavement, others are relevant to grieving personal loss, including trauma.
- The Center for Loss and Life Transition is dedicated to helping people who are grieving, and the center's website provides information about grief and loss (https://www.centerforloss.com).

Print Resources

- *Progressing Through Grief: Guided Exercises to Understand Your Emotions and Recover From Loss*, by Stephanie Jose (Althea Press, 2016). This workbook focuses on six emotions in grief—sadness, anger, guilt, anxiety, disbelief, and shame—and contains many exercises with space for journaling. Although directed primarily to bereavement, the content is relevant to losses suffered through trauma.
- *Transforming Grief & Loss Workbook*, by Ligia Houben (PESI Publishing, 2017). This workbook contains many activities and exercises for working through grief and loss; examples are "Live Your Grief" and "Express Your Feelings." Although bereavement is a focus, the book also explains grief from life transitions and from loss.

CHAPTER 6

MEANING

Recovery Milestones

This chapter will help you

1. **understand** the concept of meaning, or meaning in life;
2. **define** how trauma threatens meaning; and
3. **explain** how meaning making contributes to recovery and to well-being.

What is the meaning of "meaning"? The word is used to indicate the sense of something; you might say, "no, I didn't mean that" when someone takes what you said in a way you did not intend. Meaning can also denote significance or mattering; when someone gives you a "meaningful glance," it signals that something is important. Meaning can also indicate worth or value; that is the case when we speak of something, such as a special vacation, as "meaningful." My focus in this chapter is on "meaning in life," which is a deeper state of meaning in which life events make sense and connect toward a broader purpose. Many psychologists, as you will discover in this chapter, have emphasized the importance of meaning in life and have developed models of its relationship to well-being.

WHAT IS MEANING IN LIFE?

We are indebted to Viktor Frankl for our contemporary focus on the role of meaning. Frankl was a Jewish psychiatrist in Vienna who believed in the importance of meaning in life and its connection to social reform. He focused on helping adolescents and set up specialized counseling centers for them. In 1938, when Germany invaded Austria, he was forced to give up his practice, although he continued to work with patients in a Jewish-only clinic. In 1942, he and his family were arrested and taken to the Theresienstadt concentration camp near Prague. He later was selected for a work group on his arrival at Auschwitz. He survived the war but learned afterward that his wife and his family did not.

Frankl (1946/1992) wrote *Man's Search for Meaning*, first published in Germany in 1946, to explain the importance of meaning. In it, he described his struggle to maintain meaning or purpose in life in the concentration camps, where brutality was constant and survival virtually impossible. He wrote graphically of the torture, starvation, and murder of prisoners. His observation was that "everything can be taken from a man but one thing: the last of the human freedoms—to choose one's attitude in any given set of circumstances, to choose one's own way" (p. 75).

Frankl also observed survivors after the war because he was interested in how they created meaning of their traumatic past experiences. He saw them create meaning in three ways. One way was that they made a difference in the world through their actions or creations. A second way was that they experienced something in an intense way, such as loving another person. A third way was that they had a courageous attitude in the face of unavoidable suffering.

We can think about meaning by considering it in the context of our autobiographical memory. When we recall memories from the past, we do not retrieve a memory in isolation. Rather, we usually retrieve the memory as we weave a narrative or a story. The memories "mean something." Often, those stories are not just for the purpose of describing the past; rather, we create those stories to increase our understanding of ourselves, to make a point about our life, and to present ourselves in a particular way to ourselves or to another. In other words, we use those stories to create a "narrative identity." Our *narrative identity* is our attempt at a coherent, personal life story. It is a story about us, about how we came to be the way we are. We create meaning as we develop a theme or a "plot"—that is, as we describe the sequence of events in our personal story. That meaning may be one of productive growth, in which negative events have affected our self, but crisis created change. Or that meaning may be one of victimization and despair, in which we struggle and fail to make sense of our many losses. Either way, we approach the meaning process by thinking and processing, by resolving events into a coherent theme, and by rehearsing that story. If you wrote a story about your life as you read Chapter 3, go back to that story now. Reread it to see whether you were creating meaning as you developed the story. What is the narrative identity you see now in that story?

Crystal Park, a psychologist who studies meaning in life, believes that meaning consists of three distinct parts (George & Park, 2016). The first is comprehension. *Comprehension* is present when we have a sense of coherence, or things "hanging together," in our lives. If we have comprehension, things make sense to us; if we do not have comprehension, our life feels fragmented. Comprehension also involves coherence across time, in which distinct parts of our life feel connected.

The second part is purpose. *Purpose* is present when we have valued life goals that direct and motivate our lives. People with purpose have a clear sense of where they are trying to go, of where their path is leading; they feel pulled toward their goals. In contrast, people without purpose feel aimless and lost, and their lives appear disengaged.

The third part of meaning is mattering. *Mattering* is present when we believe that our existence is important, that we bring value to our world. When we believe we matter, we believe our existence is significant, is valuable, and has merit. Mattering is the experience that others are interested in us, depend on us, and have concern for our problems. Not mattering is the belief that we have no value, that no one outside of us depends on us or finds us important enough to seek out.

One reason psychologists are so focused on understanding meaning in life is that it is very important to our well-being. Recall from Chapter 3 the model of well-being presented by psychologist Carol Ryff (1989). She defined six aspects of happiness, of which purpose in life was one. She described purpose in life as the belief that one's life holds meaning. Martin Seligman (2018), a pioneer of positive psychology (see Chapter 3), further tied meaning in life to happiness with his PERMA model, in which happiness consists of Meaning as well as Positive emotions, Engagement, Relationships, and Accomplishments.

Research has shown that having meaning is correlated with psychological benefits, and that the absence of meaning is correlated with psychological difficulties. People who have a strong sense that life is meaningful endure less negative impact from stressors of life. People without that strong sense of life's meaning, purpose, and value suffer more from depression and anxiety. For example, three researchers interested in how happiness and meaning in life relate to mental health studied 284 university students who completed questionnaires about meaning, happiness, perceived stress, anxiety, and depression (Li et al., 2019). The researchers found that participants who had strong meaning in life had lower levels of stress, anxiety, and depression.

The positive effects of having meaning in life are more than simply psychological. Research has shown that having a sense of purpose and having coherence are linked to better physical health, including lower risk of disability and more positive perceptions of one's health (Hooker et al., 2018; Roepke et al., 2014). Evidence is accumulating that meaning in life is linked to reduced mortality, slower cognitive decline, and lower risk for heart disease. The pathways between meaning in life and these physical health outcomes are not clear, although it seems that having meaning in life leads to more health-promoting behaviors (such as exercise) as well as lower levels of stress. Insights From Psychology 6.1 presents the results of a study of meaning in life and brain health.

An interesting and important question is how meaning in life comes about. Is it present, and some people have more of it than others? Or is it searched for, so that anyone can find meaning in their lives? Or is it somehow built or constructed? This question is especially important for us in this chapter as we consider how trauma affects meaning. In one study, 250 young adults wrote in a diary every day for 2 weeks about their well-being (for example, satisfaction with life, positive emotions, self-esteem) and meaning in life (Newman et al., 2018). Those who reported that they had searched for meaning did find meaning, and the presence of meaning was associated with positive well-being in the days that followed. It seems that meaning can be increased through activities associated with searching for it, such as keeping a journal.

Russo-Netzer (2018) conducted two studies with 300 adults to understand how prioritizing meaning in life was related to well-being. The assumption behind this research was that people vary in their approach to valuing meaning in life, from a general orientation to definite intentions. They found differences in the degree to which these adults prioritized meaning. Those who highly valued meaning sought to increase their experiences of meaning, which in

Insights From Psychology 6.1

How Does Meaning in Life Affect Brain Health?

As the population ages, questions about brain health and disease in later life are becoming more important. For example, Alzheimer's disease, a disease of the brain, is currently the third leading cause of death. The concept of cognitive reserve suggests that people differ in how they experience brain-related declines because they have different amounts of cognitive reserve. *Cognitive reserve* is the mind's resistance to damage and disease, and it consists of both biological and psychological components.

In a prospective (long-term) study of more than 1,000 adults, researchers investigated whether and how meaning in life affected cognitive reserve (Bartrés-Faz et al., 2018). They measured meaning in life in three ways, using concepts we've seen in this chapter. The first was level of purpose, comprehension, and significance. The second was sense of coherence, including the confidence that one can meet demands posed by challenges in life. The third focused on engagement in life, or the degree to which one participates in meaningful and valued activities. Cognitive reserve and cognitive function (which includes memory, attention, reasoning) were also measured.

The findings revealed the importance of meaning in life for improving brain health. Meaning in life was associated with emotional well-being, with more meaning leading to less anxiety and depression. Meaning in life was also associated with improved cognitive function as shown in measures of memory, attention, and reasoning. Bartrés-Faz et al. (2018) believed that their findings suggest an important role for meaning in life as people age: Higher meaning, including purpose and coherence, may help protect people against brain disease.

turn led to well-being, including positive emotions and more life satisfaction.

In summary, here is what we know about meaning in life:

- *Meaning in life* is the extent to which we experience our lives as making sense (coherence), as motivated by important goals (purpose), and as valuable (mattering).
- People who report that their lives have meaning also experience better psychological and physical health.
- Although meaning in life is known to promote both well-being and happiness, people differ in how much they value it.

WHAT ARE THREATS TO MEANING IN LIFE?

Although meaning in life can be valued, and although its benefits have been shown, it is not immune to threats. Psychologist Crystal Park (2010) developed a model (that is, a picture of how something works and what its parts are) for how events threaten meaning, and the usefulness of this model has been supported by scientific studies. According to this model, there are two types of meaning: global and situational. *Global meanings* are our general orienting systems and assumptions about the world. Examples of such assumptions are that we are good people who receive what we deserve and that life is not random; these assumptions encompass the orienting systems of justice, predictability, coherence, and control. *Situational meanings* are our evaluations of specific events, including whether the event was threatening, why the event happened, and how the event might affect our future. When the global meaning and the situational meaning do not match, there is dissonance: *Dissonance* is the tension we experience when different elements of meaning are not harmonious, when they do not fit well together.

Consider the example of a parent who believes in a just world but then experiences the sudden death of their child from a rare illness. In a just world (global meaning), loving parents do not suddenly lose a child to a rare illness (situational meaning). The parent can conclude that the world is not just, reducing the dissonance by changing the global meaning to match the situational meaning. When a global meaning changes, however, it is not changed only for the specific event, but rather is a comprehensive change, meaning that in the future, the parent will continue to believe that the world is unjust. Alternatively, the parent can reduce dissonance by concluding that even though the child's death will forever be painful, they can respond to the crisis by making some changes consistent with the value they place on the global meaning of a just world. For example, the parent might become an advocate for children with the rare disease and unite their parents in a supportive online peer group. Going forward, the parent can address the threat to meaning by both seeing the world as just (same global meaning) and acknowledging that the child's death has brought about an opportunity to help others (new situational meaning).

Changes in global or situational meanings are called "meanings made," and the thought processes that bring about these changes are called "meaning making." We make many different meanings after resolving dissonance. For example, cancer survivors interviewed 1 year and 3 years after their treatment were asked whether the crises of their diagnosis and treatment had brought about positive change, a form of meaning making (Tallman et al., 2007). These survivors had received a bone marrow transplant, a treatment that is demanding both physically (for example, fever, skin disease, mouth sores) and psychologically (for example, isolation). They mentioned several changes; examples were having a new perspective on life, building a life with new directions (including career changes), and experiencing improved interpersonal relationships. Participants who identified changes 1 year after treatment were significantly less depressed 3 years after treatment than those who were unable to identify changes.

There are important questions about the process of meaning making. First, how common is it for people to attempt to find meaning? In an analysis of many studies, Park (2010) found that most people, 60% to 75%, searched for meaning after experiencing a difficult or challenging event. Second, how common is it for people to report they actually found meaning after searching for it? Across studies, many people reported finding meaning, although fewer than those who searched for meaning. However, a substantial number of people reported that they had not succeeded in finding meaning after a difficult event.

How does one make meaning after a traumatic event? Traumas such as natural disasters, industrial disasters, mass shootings, and motor vehicle accidents pose significant challenges to the physical and psychosocial health of those who experience them. For example, an estimated 30% to 40% of people who survive a disaster show symptoms of posttraumatic stress disorder in the aftermath of the event (Neria et al., 2008). And by definition, traumas challenge survivors' global meanings because they shatter assumptions about the benevolence of people, the fairness and predictability of events, and the worth of the self. Traumas are often a marker dividing people's lives into "before" and "after."

Recall that meaning making begins when we evaluate situational meanings; traumas create situational meanings of threat and loss. Global meanings are challenged as well because the trauma would not have occurred in a world that is characterized by order, fairness, and benevolence. Meaning making after trauma is likely to require changes in global meanings—for example, regarding the likelihood of evil in a fair and just world or the likelihood that one can exercise control over one's life. Meaning making after trauma usually includes making some sense of the event, accepting the difficulties it presents, and making crisis-related change. Another way people create meaning after trauma is through the construction of a new identity that integrates the trauma. In summary, here is what we know about threats to meaning:

- Threats to meaning arise when global meanings are contradicted by the situational meanings attached to events.
- People resolve that contradiction, or dissonance, by changing global meanings, situational meanings, or both.
- "Meaning made" is the outcome of the struggle to reconcile the contradictory global meanings and situational meanings.

MEANING MAKING AND CHILDHOOD SEXUAL ABUSE

A question that may have occurred to you while reading this chapter is how to make meaning of the trauma of sexual abuse while you were a child. If you consider your life using the meaning making model, you might wonder whether you made meanings as a child. We will focus on meaning making as an adult later in this section, but before we do, let's consider research on how children engage in meaning making about their abuse. Three clinician–researchers studied 108 children ages 8 to 15 years who had been sexually abused to determine whether and how they tried to make meaning of those events (Simon et al., 2010). The participants joined the study after they disclosed their abuse and became involved in legal proceedings against the perpetrator. Six years later, these youth participated in follow-up interviews about their experiences.

After analyzing the interview responses, the researchers defined three outcomes, or results, of the youths' meaning-making efforts (Simon et al., 2010). The first is the "constructive" outcome.

Fourteen percent of the youth were still processing their abuse memories, but they had been able to construct more adaptive—that is, helpful—meanings of their experience, such as by making sense of the event, finding some benefit, or seeing it in a different way. The constructive outcome was associated with less anxiety and fewer intrusive memories. The second is the "avoidant" outcome. Thirty-six percent of the youth had completely disengaged from their abuse history, made no effort to think about the impact of the abuse on their lives, and minimized the abuse. This outcome was associated with more symptoms of depression and dissociation. The third is the "absorbed" outcome. Fifty percent of these youth continued to try to process their experiences but were not able to do so productively. They became overwhelmed and angry, and they showed the most depression and shame of all the participants.

Why might the youth with avoidant and absorbed outcomes have experienced difficulties in making meaning? We don't know exactly why; it is still something that research has not been able to answer. But betrayal blindness is the best solution to date, because it applies to virtually all childhood sexual abuse. Recall the concept of betrayal blindness from Chapter 2. If you did not read that chapter, here is a summary of the concept: Sexual abuse is more than a trauma; it is an act in which the child is betrayed by a trusted and valued person. Thus, the abuse is a betrayal of the relationship between the child and a perpetrator who was a parent, family member, close friend, or trusted adult. The great difficulty for the child is that he or she cannot escape from the relationship. Thus, the child develops betrayal blindness: an inability to remember the events, a persistent benign ("not that big a deal") or self-blaming view of the events, or even the belief that the events were normal. This blindness allows the child to remain in the relationship, but it carries the consequences of shame, depression, physical symptoms, and dissociation.

Betrayal blindness interferes with the development of meaning because meaning creation or construction rests on being able to think clearly about events (situational meaning) and one's global meanings. When children create meaning about themselves and their experiences, they try to integrate what appear to be contradictions into a coherent and even complex story. If they cannot achieve that integration, they have large gaps in their memory, and the memories they do have can be recalled only under certain contexts.

The first research study conducted specifically to understand adult meaning making after childhood sexual abuse was carried out by three psychologists in the early 1980s, at a time when childhood sexual abuse was first being recognized as a significant and frequent occurrence (Silver et al., 1983). Their participants were 77 women who had experienced incest as children, beginning at an average age of 8 years. The study took place an average of 20 years after the abuse had ended. Despite that distance, more than 80% of the women reported still searching for meaning, and the same number indicated that making sense of their abuse was still important to them. The women who reported still searching for meaning reported more distress, lower self-esteem, and less confidence in interpersonal relationships than women who no longer searched for meaning, either because they had found meaning or had never attempted to define meaning. Searching for meaning over a lengthy period of time thus appears to be associated with poor outcomes, and it actually seems better not to search than to search for a long time and not find meaning.

Recall that change after crisis is one important aspect of meaning making; if one can have positive changes after crisis, the situational meaning is improved. The specific question of whether people can experience positive change after childhood sexual abuse was considered by three psychologists who interviewed 154 women about their experience (McMillen et al., 1995). They found that almost half of the participants reported positive changes, including believing they were better able to protect their own children from abuse, experiencing internal changes such as learning to trust their instincts, having more empathy with other survivors, and believing they were stronger because of their abuse. Self-Assessment 6.1 gives you a way of beginning the process of meaning making for yourself.

Self-Assessment 6.1

How Do You Make Meaning?

This exercise is modified from a directed journaling technique by Lichtenthal and Neimeyer (2012). Write in your journal or note-taking app for at least 15 minutes on at least three or four separate occasions. On each occasion, write freely about either the way you make sense of the abuse or the changes you made after it, and write as much or as little as you like. Don't go back and review what you have written until you complete all the occasions for writing. Then reread your journaling and write a summary of what you have learned.

Sense Making

Sense making is answering questions about why the abuse occurred and what effects of that experience have carried over into your adult life. Try to write about the basic question of how the abuse fits or does not fit into your global meanings. Here are questions to get you started:

1. How have you made sense of the abuse in the past? Did you try to make sense of it as a child or adolescent?
2. How do you make sense of the abuse now?
3. Did the abuse have an effect on your core beliefs about the world or about yourself? How did those beliefs change?
4. How has the abuse affected your life?
5. If you could put yourself 10 years into the future, how would the abuse affect your life then?

(continues)

Self-Assessment 6.1 (*Continued*)

Changes After Crisis

Think about changes after the crisis of your abuse (or another crisis) when you found a positive significance or positive effects in particular areas of your life. Try to write about positive changes, such as in your life goals, interpersonal relationships, or how you see yourself. Here are questions to get you started:

1. Has the abuse resulted in changes to your identity? If it has, what are those changes, and are they positive or negative?
2. What are things that people say are the best parts of you? Did the abuse have any effect on those things?
3. Are there life lessons you have learned from the abuse?

In a study of meaning making by 60 women who had been sexually abused as children, 50% of the participants reported positive changes from their experiences (Wright et al., 2007). The researchers found six categories of positive change: personal growth, spiritual growth, increased knowledge of sexual abuse, improved relationships with others, newly acquired coping skills, and improved parenting skills. They also found that 32% of the participants described shattered assumptions about the world (for example, justice and fairness), 14% described shattered beliefs about themselves, and 29% said they had made or found no meaning. These results provide evidence that for some people, the process of meaning making may still not be complete even after many years. Insights From Psychology 6.2 summarizes a study that examined how resilient male survivors of childhood sexual abuse from a range of ethnic, racial, and socioeconomic backgrounds made meaning from their experience.

Insights From Psychology 6.2

Meaning Making by Male Survivors of Childhood Sexual Abuse

Much of the research on meaning making after abuse has been conducted with women. But being victimized by childhood sexual abuse is not an experience confined to women. A national survey found that 16% of men reported having experienced childhood sexual abuse before age 18 (Dube et al., 2005). We know, too, from nationally publicized incidents that some team doctors for male athletic teams and some clergy and other religious authorities have abused many victims over many years. Therefore, it is important to understand the male experience of childhood sexual abuse. Grossman and colleagues (2006) conducted interviews with 16 men (10 White, two African American, three Latino, and one Native American) about their meaning making after childhood sexual abuse.

Most of the men described making meaning through altruistic or advocacy behaviors and creative expressions about the abuse. For example, some built a vocation around helping others as counselors and mental health volunteers. Many of the men made meaning through thought or reason. Some of them explained the abuse by focusing on the perpetrator, trying to find a way to understand their actions. Others focused on trying to understand their own role; some blamed themselves for the abuse, a meaning making method that is not helpful. The third type of meaning making was developing their spirituality. Only two of the men were involved in organized religion, but about half had constructed spiritual ways of being, for example through involvement in AA or another 12-step program.

The authors noted that most of the men reported engaging in self-blame, a greater percentage than in samples of women; and this finding may reflect these men's struggle with the masculine values of strength and power that were violated by the abuse. Psychologists know that for survivors of childhood sexual abuse, self-blame is a way of restoring the orderliness of the world (global meaning); essentially, by considering themselves responsible for the abuse, survivors claim a measure of control over their lives. But self-blame in adulthood is associated with the

(continues)

> **Insights From Psychology 6.2 (*Continued*)**
>
> negative emotions of shame, doubt, fear, and depression. Self-blame leads to the experience of an "inner critic"—a part of oneself whose messages are negative "shoulds" such as "you should be over this by now," disparaging statements such as "your behavior is an embarrassment to your family," and negative predictions such as "your life will always be a mess." Those messages from the inner critic lead to feelings of worthlessness and shame.

In summary, here is what we know about meaning making after childhood sexual abuse:

- Data from adolescents and adults show that meaning making is a difficult part of recovery from childhood sexual abuse.
- Meaning making is associated with the positive outcomes of emotional health and physical health.
- It is hard to know how many adults search for and find meaning, given different definitions of that concept across studies, but one conclusion from this research is that most adults do search for meaning after their abuse.
- Finding meaning consists of making sense of the abuse in the larger context of life and identifying positive and durable change after crisis.

MEANING MAKING REVISITED

No matter where you are on your meaning-making journey, here are four ways you can start or keep going toward the goal of finding meaning. First, acknowledge that all of your experiences teach you about yourself. Do you ever think that you are "on the path" or "off the path"? I certainly do. If I wake up in the morning and reflect that I used avoidant coping methods the day before for whatever the stressor was, I think to myself that I am way off the path. But thinking this prevents us from learning. You are always on your path! All experiences, good and bad, teach you. Second, put your life in a larger context; Self-Assessment 6.2 will help you begin that process. Third, ask others what they value in you as a way of learning about yourself. This information is essential in meaning making, which rests on accurate perceptions, not the totally negative view of self that many victims have. It may seem weird to ask that question of a friend, and you may not have friends you would be comfortable asking. But if possible, see what others say about what they value in you. Last, find or create meaning by giving of yourself to others or to a value or a passion.

Self-Assessment 6.2

Mountains and Valleys

This exercise is modified from "The Mountain Range Exercise" in Pattakos and Dundon (2017). Imagine your life as a series of mountains and valleys. Then draw the good parts of your life as mountains and the difficult times as valleys using large stretches of newsprint or on a note-taking or drawing app. Label the positive experiences and supportive people on the mountains. Label the negative experiences and abusive people in the valleys.

Look at all the mountains. Is there a common theme across your mountains? Did the mountains simply happen, or was there something you did that helped build the mountains? What did you learn from the mountains over time? Write your answers in your journal or note-taking app.

Then look at all the valleys. Is there a common theme across your valleys? Did they happen to you without your control, or were you able to influence them? What have you learned from the valleys? Write your answers in your journal or note-taking app.

RESOURCES

- *Prisoners of Our Thoughts*, by Alex Pattakos and Elaine Dundon (Berrett Koehler Publishers, 2017). This book expands on the writings of Viktor Frankl and describes how to follow a series of core principles on meaning: choose your attitude, assume responsibility for making meaning, and become the person you want to be. The book contains many exercises and directed readings.

- *The Gifts of Imperfection: Let Go of Who You Think You're Supposed to Be and Embrace Who You Are*, by Brené Brown (Hazelden Publishing, 2010). Brené Brown is the author of many widely read books about authentic living. This book explains why letting go of commitments such as perfectionism and approval seeking from others is necessary for courage and self-compassion.

- *The Reality Slap: Finding Peace and Fulfillment When Life Hurts*, by Russ Harris (New Harbinger, 2012). This book confronts straight-on the life experiences of crises and pain. The author focuses on finding peace, understanding difficult emotions, and healing wounds. There are exercises and self-assessments.

CHAPTER 7

SPIRITUALITY

Recovery Milestones

This chapter will help you

1. **define** the related but different concepts of spirituality and religiosity;
2. **examine** how spirituality and religiosity are damaged by childhood sexual abuse; and
3. **understand** your own sense of spirituality, including spiritual struggles and spiritual fortitude.

What is "soul murder"? The term was introduced by playwright Henrick Ibsen, who defined it as the destruction of the love of life in another human being. The outcome of this is a person without an authentic identity and without the ability to experience joy in life. The damage is to the soul, the essence of the person. The term "soul murder" has been applied to the experience of childhood sexual abuse, which leaves the child's body intact but destroys their spirit. Is this your experience? It was mine, and when I learned the concept of soul murder, it explained the great darkness in my life. It is because of the evil done to abuse victims that the concept of spirituality is so important. Survivors have been damaged not just in their mind and body, but also in their spirit.

WHAT IS SPIRITUALITY, AND WHAT IS RELIGIOSITY?

Psychologists have dramatically increased their study of spirituality and religiosity. To do that successfully, they needed clear definitions of both concepts. Three researchers reviewed more than 500 published studies to find characteristics that researchers agree differentiate spirituality from religiosity (Harris et al., 2018). The definitions of these characteristics may be helpful as you consider your own experiences of spirituality and religiosity. Spirituality is composed of the following characteristics:

- *Internal emphasis:* Spirituality is internal in nature, a state of being within the individual that creates a sense of peace and fulfillment.
- *Ultimate concerns:* Spirituality is concerned with transcendence—with values and purposes that are larger than everyday life.
- *Self-enhancement:* People grow when they accept that their heart and mind are connected to the natural world.

Religiosity is composed of the following:

- *Beliefs:* The core of religiosity is understanding and following sets of beliefs—beliefs about the divine (meaning of, from, or like God), about humanity, and about the interaction of humanity with the divine.
- *Rituals:* Religiosity involves participation in rituals that are communal (that is, shared within a community) and rituals that are private.
- *Behaviors:* Religiosity includes behaviors that fulfill codes of ethical and moral behavior—for example, providing charity to those in need within the faith group and in the larger community.

In this chapter, *spirituality* is the deep experience of connectedness to the sacred (meaning connected with God) or the divine, a personal focus on spiritual interests, and activities connected to ultimate significance. *Religiosity* is a commitment to and beliefs about God or a deity that create a meaning framework, promote participation in religious behaviors, and motivate adherence to beliefs and practices. Take a minute and in your journal or note-taking app, write down how you see yourself right now in relation to spirituality, first, and then in relation to religiosity.

Spirituality and religiosity are not something one "has." Rather, they are best viewed as a relationship between oneself and the divine. This concept goes back to William James, a pioneering psychologist who studied religion in the early 1900s. He defined "personal religion" as "feelings, acts, and experiences of individual men [and women] in their solitude, so far as they apprehend themselves to stand in relation to whatever they may consider as divine" (James, 1902, p. 42). Religiosity and spirituality are also both about connections. We connect with ourselves, we connect with others and with nature, and we connect with transcendence. People who are religious see the connection with transcendence as a connection with God or a deity, or with a faith community of people who share values and practices, or with historical figures such as saints, or with visual representations such as icons. Other connections may be with figures in their own past, such as relatives now dead.

To summarize, here is what we know about spirituality and religiosity:

- Spirituality is a concern with the transcendent, with an internal state of relating to oneself, to nature, to the divine.
- Religiosity is concerned with belief and actions, adherence to codes of ethical and moral behavior, and practices driven by the value of caring for others in a faith community and outside it.

- Both spirituality and religiosity have to do with connections between us and ourselves, other people, the world around us, and the transcendent.

HOW ARE SPIRITUALITY AND RELIGIOSITY RELATED TO WELL-BEING?

Spirituality and religiosity begin their influence in adolescence. During the past 20 years, more than 600 published studies have considered religiosity and spirituality among adolescents. The most frequent finding is that adolescents benefit from a strong sense of spirituality or a strong commitment to religiosity, or both, and exhibit fewer risky behaviors and better mental health than adolescents who have no or little spirituality and religiosity. For example, a large sample of adolescents (16,000) provided information on religiosity and on various mental health outcomes (Nonnemaker et al., 2003). Those who had stronger religiosity were more likely to experience better mental health, fewer suicide attempts, and fewer risky behaviors (e.g., substance use and abuse).

Among adults, research on the question of well-being has focused on behaviors or attitudes or both. For example, a study of 470 adults considered how religiousness was related to positive well-being (Dezutter et al., 2006). The psychologists used measures that allowed them to compare religious behaviors to religious attitudes. Religious behaviors, such as church attendance, did not appear to influence participants' well-being. But those with stronger religious affiliations (attitudes) showed more positive emotions and lower distress.

Much of the research on well-being has focused on people from specific populations, such as young adults, combat veterans, persons with cancer, or older adults. For example, a study of a national sample of 9,500 college students (Nadal et al., 2018) divided participants into four groups—religious and spiritual, religious but not spiritual, spiritual but not religious, and neither religious nor spiritual—and compared the groups in terms of positive outcomes (such as identity maturity and psychological health and well-being) and negative outcomes (such as depression, antisocial behavior, and sexual risk taking). Students who were both religious and spiritual had the fewest negative outcomes and the most positive outcomes, and those who were religious but not spiritual had the most negative outcomes; the other two groups fell in the middle.

By what mechanisms do religiosity and spirituality affect positive well-being? There have been many ideas about this relationship. One set of ideas are that people who are religious receive social support from their faith community, use coping strategies such as prayer and reading religious articles, and have a direct and helpful relationship with a religious leader. This mechanism presumes that religious involvement in a community of like-minded individuals provides the same type of positive support as other community memberships.

Another idea for a mechanism is that spirituality and religiosity influence meaning in life. If you have not read Chapter 6 yet, here is a summary: Meaning in life occurs when three characteristics are present. The first is comprehension. *Comprehension* is when events make sense, when things "hang together" in our lives. The second is purpose. When we have *purpose* in life, we have valued life goals that motivate and direct us. The third is mattering. *Mattering* is when we believe that our existence is important and that we bring value to our world. Religious and spiritual people experience more meaning in life as they engage in activities such as meditating, attending religious services, and caring for others in a faith context (such as volunteering for a food bank with others from one's church, synagogue, or mosque). These activities arise from a sense of purpose in life and create a greater experience of meaning that results in better psychological and physical health.

Biological pathways are another mechanism through which religiosity and spirituality are believed to affect well-being. In a review of published research, three psychologists identified practices that belong to religious or spiritual traditions and the physical health effects of those practices (Seeman et al., 2003). In the category of religious practices, behaviors such as attending religious services and reading religious texts were associated with lower blood pressure, improved hypertension (high blood pressure), and healthier immune function. In the category of spiritual practices, meditation was associated with less reactivity to stress and better physical health outcomes in people diagnosed with diseases. The authors concluded that although more data are needed, spirituality and religiosity are clearly linked to physiological processes that lead to better health.

To summarize, here is what we know about the effects of spirituality and religiosity:

- Both spirituality and religiosity result in better psychosocial and physical outcomes among adolescents and adults.
- The mechanisms or pathways by which this improvement is obtained are unclear. It may be that meaning in life is affected by both religiosity and spirituality and that improved meaning is linked to better outcomes. There may also be physical processes such as hormones or immune function that are involved.

HOW DOES TRAUMA DAMAGE SPIRITUALITY AND RELIGIOSITY?

Challenges to spirituality and religiosity are common among survivors of a trauma such as a natural disaster or the violent loss of a loved one. Our global meanings, even if we are not religious, express our deeply held assumptions about justice in the world, fairness, and personal worth. Suffering can call forth questions about the role of a deity, even if the person who suffers has not been religious. One often hears "Where was God when this was happening? How can a loving God allow this to happen?" even from people who had not engaged in religious activities before the trauma. For people who have strong religious beliefs or deep spiritual connections, the trauma shakes the foundations that have been in place.

One example of a personal trauma is bereavement. The loss of a loved one, even if it was expected and logical ("they lived a good life"), is challenging. An unexpected, violent, or shattering death (such as the death of a child) creates significantly more distress. Bereavement is a loss of connection, both to the lost one and often to one's community as well. A review of published studies found that religiosity and spirituality were helpful after bereavement (Wortmann & Park, 2008). Specifically, general religiousness (attitudes), use of positive religious coping, and behaviors such as participation in church services and other organized activities were beneficial.

Another example of a personal trauma is living through a natural disaster. Natural disasters threaten one's home, livelihood, and future, along with personal safety and the safety of one's family and community. It is not uncommon for survivors to have symptoms consistent with posttraumatic stress disorder, and for those symptoms to last over time. Spirituality expressed in meaning making may be a buffer for those losses. *Spiritual meaning* is a deep sense of coherence, purpose, and mattering drawn from religious or spiritual beliefs. Spiritual meanings can help protect survivors against the stresses of disaster.

The trauma we focus on in this book is a childhood trauma. The trauma of childhood sexual abuse is at the center of our narrative, but all childhood traumas affect spirituality and religiosity. Insights From Psychology 7.1 presents a study of adults who experienced childhood trauma that examined their current religiosity and spirituality.

Insights From Psychology 7.1

Adult Spirituality After Childhood Trauma

The experience of childhood trauma—emotional abuse, physical abuse, sexual abuse, emotional neglect, or physical neglect—has been shown to affect adult religiosity and spirituality. Most research on this topic examined primarily religious participants, as opposed to nonreligious participants, and was conducted in countries that were primarily religious; this type of study allowed researchers to examine religion as separate from spirituality. But we're interested in both. A study of 1,800 adults in the Czech Republic, a secular country, provided information regarding their childhood traumas and their current religiosity and spirituality. The researchers were public health scientists (Kosarkova et al., 2020).

The study showed that people who had experienced childhood trauma were more likely to be spiritual but not religious. This was true for sexual abuse as well: Adults who had been sexually abused as children were more likely to be spiritual but not religious rather than any of the other categories. The authors suggested that being religious may make it difficult for people to assimilate a childhood trauma; the trauma challenges a belief in a deity or higher power that is benevolent, and survivors often conclude that the deity or higher power abandoned or punished them.

Recall that one outcome of trauma can be posttraumatic growth. If you have not read Chapter 3, here is a brief summary: After the difficulties of a trauma, people may experience enduring positive changes in several specific areas. One area is changed perceptions of self—for example, seeing oneself as stronger and more capable. A second area is improvements in interpersonal relationships. A third area is new directions in life, such as occupational changes. A fourth area is increased spirituality. A fifth area is changes in life philosophy—for example, appreciating the small things in life.

A review of published studies about how religion and spirituality contribute to posttraumatic growth after trauma was carried out by researchers in the United Kingdom (Shaw et al., 2005). They found that women with abuse and trauma histories who were spiritual reported that their spirituality was a positive resource for them in adulthood and that it had contributed to their posttraumatic growth. But religious participants who engaged in negative religious coping after their trauma did not experience posttraumatic growth. Negative religious coping includes self-blame, feeling that one has been punished or abandoned by God or a deity, and doubting or questioning one's religious beliefs. Posttraumatic growth follows a period of struggle, so it may be that these participants' religious beliefs interfered with their ability to fully carry out that struggle.

Another way that spirituality plays a role after trauma is through spiritual transformation. *Spiritual transformation* consists of enduring changes in one's spirituality and its expression and can result in either a gain or a decline. Spiritual gain is experienced as a greater sense of gratitude and more frequent connection to the spiritual through rituals, readings, and meditation. Spiritual decline is experienced as being spiritually "shut down," not knowing what to believe anymore, feeling spiritually wounded, and feeling spiritually lost. Spiritual gain after a trauma is often reflected in the increased importance of spirituality to the person, whereas spiritual decline is expressed as persistent distress and anger about the trauma.

Spiritual struggles can follow trauma for both people who are religious and those who are not. These struggles increase anxiety, which sets off a search for change in how they relate to the sacred or transcendent in the context of the trauma. Spiritual gains are likely to be discontinuous; that is, they often do not occur smoothly over time but rather are vivid, surprising alterations. Self-Assessment 7.1 is a test that can help you understand your own experience with spiritual struggles.

To summarize, here is what we know about how stressors and trauma affect spirituality and religiosity:

- Stressors and trauma create challenges to both spirituality and religiosity.
- Those challenges happen because our global meanings are contradicted by the trauma and by the accompanying losses of a physical and psychosocial nature.
- Spirituality and religiosity can provide us with resources for coping with stressors and trauma.
- A primary pathway for the influence of spirituality and religiosity on posttraumatic growth is through meaning making; a secondary pathway is through spiritual transformation.

SPIRITUALITY AND RELIGIOSITY AFTER CHILDHOOD SEXUAL ABUSE

The earliest research on the damages caused by childhood sexual abuse was done with adult survivors who had a religious upbringing (Russell, 1999). This research, conducted in the 1990s, when a religious upbringing was more common, yielded two conclusions. The first was that childhood sexual abuse led to a decrease in experiences of religiosity and spirituality in adulthood. For example, one study of women who had been sexually abused by a father figure found that 60% had rejected any practice of religion (T. A. Hall, 1995). A second conclusion was that among women sexually abused as children who were still affiliated with a church, their practice of faith-related attitudes and behaviors was significantly lower, even

Self-Assessment 7.1

Spiritual Struggles

The statements listed below describe struggles with spirituality. When you consider your spiritual and religious life after childhood sexual abuse, how true for you is each of these statements? In your journal or note-taking app, write down the number that indicates how accurately each statement describes how you have felt over the past month using this scale: 1 = *not at all true*, 2 = *a little bit true*, 3 = *somewhat true*, 4 = *quite a bit true*, and 5 = *a great deal true.*

1. I felt as though God had let me down.
2. I felt angry at God.
3. I felt as though God had abandoned me.
4. I felt as though God was punishing me.
5. I questioned God's love for me.
6. I felt tormented by the devil or by evil spirits.
7. I worried that problems I was facing were the work of the devil or evil spirits.
8. I felt attacked by the devil or evil spirits.
9. I felt as though the devil (or an evil spirit) was trying to turn me away from what was good.
10. I felt hurt, mistreated, or offended by religious or spiritual people.
11. I felt rejected or misunderstood by religious or spiritual people.
12. I felt as though others were looking down on me because of my spiritual beliefs.
13. I had conflicts with other people about religious or spiritual matters.
14. I felt angry at organized religion.
15. I wrestled with attempts to follow my moral principles.
16. I worried that my actions were morally or spiritually wrong.
17. I felt torn between what I wanted and what I knew was morally right.
18. I felt guilty for not living up to my moral standards.
19. I questioned whether my life really matters.
20. I felt as though my life has no deeper meaning.
21. I questioned whether my life will really make a difference in the world.

(continues)

Self-Assessment 7.1 (Continued)

22. I had concerns about whether there is any ultimate purpose to life or existence.
23. I struggled to figure out what I really believe about religion and spirituality.
24. I felt confused about my religious and spiritual beliefs.
25. I felt troubled by doubts or questions about religion and spirituality.
26. I worried about whether my beliefs about religion and spirituality are correct.

Calculate your average scores in the following categories:

- Struggles concerning the divine: Items 1–5 (add your scores for these items and divide by 5)
- Struggles concerning evil: Items 6–9 (add your scores for these items and divide by 4)
- Struggles with people: Items 10–14 (add your scores for these items and divide by 5)
- Struggles over morality: Items 15–18 (add your scores for these items and divide by 4)
- Meaning-making struggles: Items 19–22 (add your scores for these items and divide by 4)
- Struggles with doubt: Items 23–26 (add your scores for these items and divide by 4).

Your average score for each category will be between 1 and 5. For adults who have not gone through trauma, the average score in each category ranges from 1.0 to 2.0. Your scores are likely to be higher.

Identify the category of struggles for which your average score is the highest. In your journal or note-taking app, write about the experiences that led you to struggle in that area and how you see those struggles playing out in your life.

though they were still church members, than those of women who had not been abused. Sexual abuse by a person with a religious commitment is particularly damaging. Abuse by a trusted adult who is also a spiritual or faith figure—priest, youth pastor, or rabbi—is uniquely traumatizing. People who are sexually abused as children in the context of a faith-informed relationship experience a *faith betrayal*: a betrayal of both the relationship and the faith or religious context. The outcomes of this trauma are debilitating and long-lasting and include damaged spiritual and religious beliefs and connections.

Over the past decade, studies of the influence of childhood sexual abuse on religiosity and spirituality have shown that for many survivors, their personal spiritual or religious life is stuck in transition as they are unable to reconcile their abuse experience with their spiritual or religious values. For some survivors, however, researchers have found that spiritual growth can occur (see the review by D. F. Walker et al., 2009). For those survivors, spirituality or religiosity helps them create meaning or gives them resources such as support in coping with difficulties. Other research has shown that the experience of childhood sexual abuse damages the individual's view of God or a deity. Many survivors have a combination of these responses; they are able to create meaning using a spiritual or religious base, and they also experience spiritual discontent. Insights From Psychology 7.2 describes a study of the role of spirituality in recovery from childhood sexual abuse.

To summarize, here is what we know about childhood sexual abuse and spirituality and religiosity:

- The effects of childhood sexual abuse on the religiosity and spirituality of adult survivors are damaged self-image and interrupted religious and spiritual development.

Insights From Psychology 7.2

What Is the Role of Spirituality in Recovery From Childhood Sexual Abuse?

Because spirituality and religiosity can help people recover from traumas and significant life stressors, it is tempting to expect that the same will happen for survivors of childhood sexual abuse. But research on this subject shows mixed results. Some survivors find their beliefs and values and practices helpful, but others have great difficulty seeing a positive role in their lives for spirituality and religiosity.

An interview-based study of 14 female survivors of childhood sexual abuse provided additional information on this topic (Houg, 2008). These survivors ranged in age from 25 to 59 and had differing racial and ethnic backgrounds, years of education, and levels of religious commitment. All of the survivors had been abused by a man who lived with the family at the time the abuse occurred, and five had been abused by more than one person.

One important finding was that the participants had difficulty having a relationship with themselves. They reported very negative views of themselves, including feeling unworthy, dirty, and deserving of the abuse. A second important finding was that the women's spirituality was an important source of positivity. Some found that their relationships with other people began to improve when they focused on their spirituality, which suggests that spirituality had a positive influence on their negative self-image. The third important finding was that the women could identify specific parts of their recovery that had to do with aspects of their spirituality, such as trust in God or a deity, anger at God or a deity, shame, and sin.

The contribution of this study was in identifying barriers to spirituality that the women saw in themselves, such as choices they made, or actions they participated in, or their unwillingness to forgive the perpetrator or family members, or their general guilt and shame. So using their spirituality to help them love themselves was a critical part of their recovery.

- Survivors struggle to reconcile their experiences with religious values, such as loving others, and with spiritual practices, such as connection and acceptance.

HOW CAN YOU USE SPIRITUALITY AND RELIGIOSITY AS RESOURCES FOR RECOVERY?

You may not be spiritually or religiously oriented at present, or you may have a strong commitment to one or the other or both. But spirituality and religiosity are important to recovery from the damage of childhood sexual abuse in three ways (Van Tongeren et al., 2019). First, building your "spiritual endurance" helps you develop the confidence that you can draw on your spirituality for help in adversity. Second, building your "spiritual enterprise" helps you believe that you have integrity and can live your life with integrity. Finally, building your sense of "redemptive purpose" gives you confidence that you will discover a sense of meaning and purpose. These three contributions have been termed *spiritual fortitude* (Van Tongeren et al., 2019). A test to measure your own spiritual fortitude is presented in Self-Assessment 7.2.

Recall why spirituality and religiosity are important resources for recovery from childhood sexual abuse: It is because childhood sexual abuse is soul murder—the taking of the joy of life from one person by another. You may or may not have actual physical scars from your abuse, but you certainly have spiritual scars. That is true whether you are religious but not spiritual, both religious and spiritual, spiritual but not religious, or neither spiritual nor religious. Those spiritual scars will fade with a sense of deep spirituality. You can deepen your spirituality by participating in activities, experiences, and beliefs that help you feel compassion, awe, gratitude, appreciation, inspiration, admiration, elevation, and love. You can do so by volunteering, by meditating, by journaling, by experiencing

Spiritual Fortitude

The statements listed below describe responses to adversity or trials. (If the term "faith" doesn't apply to you, substitute "spirituality" instead.) In your journal or note-taking app, write down how accurately each statement describes your typical way of responding to difficulties using this scale: 1 = *strongly disagree*, 2 = *disagree*, 3 = *neither agree or disagree*, 4 = *agree*, or 5 = *strongly agree*.

1. My faith helps push me to overcome difficult tasks in life.
2. I continue to do the right thing despite facing hardships.
3. Hardships give me a sense of renewed purpose.
4. My faith helps me stand up for what is right during challenging times.
5. I am able to do the right thing even in the midst of hardship.
6. My sense of purpose is strengthened through adversity.
7. My faith helps me withstand difficulties.
8. I retain my will to live despite my hardships.
9. I find meaning in my struggles.

The items form the following subscales:

- Spiritual endurance: Items 1, 4, and 7. *Spiritual endurance* is the belief that you can draw upon spiritual resources during adversity.
- Spiritual enterprise: Items 2, 5, and 8. *Spiritual enterprise* is the belief that you have integrity and that you can live your life with integrity.
- Redemptive purpose: Items 3, 6, and 9. *Redemptive purpose* is the belief that you have or will discover a meaning in life from your adversities.

The three subscales of the measure may provide you with new information on how you can use spirituality during adversity. The use of spirituality to buffer, or protect, you from negative effects of stress is one way. The use of spirituality to stimulate positive actions for others, or spill over, is another way. The last way is that spirituality allows you to lean into adversity, to accept it, to increase positive outcomes.

nature and your connection with the natural world, and by intentionally living as much as you can in community.

RESOURCES

Digital Resources

- The PositivePsychology.com website (https://positivepsychology. com/science-of-spirituality/) provides information about spirituality in everyday terminology and ideas for practices that can increase our spirituality. Particularly important are the explanations of the links between emotions and spirituality, especially the emotions of transcendence.

Print Resources

- *Falling Upward: A Spirituality for the Two Halves of Life*, by Richard Rohr (Jossey-Bass, 2011). Richard Rohr is a Franciscan priest and the founder of the Center for Action and Contemplation, and he has written many books on spirituality. This book considers how we are able to grow spiritually when we do wrong rather than right and how adversity and failure can help us gain spiritual insight.
- *The Heart of the Matter: A Workbook and Guide to Finding Your Way Back to Self-Love*, by Joffre McClung (Balboa Press, 2017). We know that childhood sexual abuse damages our ability to value ourselves. This book focuses on self-love through understanding the self and learning to value our selves that have been left behind. There are many self-assessments and exercises, along with questions to encourage directed journaling.

- *Your Surviving Spirit: A Spiritual Workbook for Coping With Trauma*, by Dusty Miller (New Harbinger, 2003). This workbook contains information, exercises, and activities that can help you use spirituality to heal from trauma. Self-assessments and space for journaling guide readers toward finding a spiritual self, setting spiritual goals, and establishing ways to engage in spiritual practices.

CHAPTER 8

CONNECTION

Recovery Milestones

This chapter will help you

1. **understand** connection and social support as recovery resources,
2. **recognize** how connection and social support function after trauma, and
3. **identify** how social support will help your recovery journey.

In California, a public health campaign proclaimed, "Friends can be good medicine." The notion that friendships with others are beneficial is something of an accepted truth. Sources as different as sports broadcasts, religious services, coffee mugs, and billboards proclaim the importance of having a friend and being a friend. Just because I was curious, I entered "friendship" on the Amazon shopping site. The search results included more than 30,000 friendship-related products. There were books and movies, bracelets, signs, and yes, even coffee mugs! Our society has elevated friendships and interpersonal relationships to a high level. This chapter shows how support from others can contribute to your recovery. But there are also difficulties and challenges in interpersonal connections that relate back to your abuse history, and I'll discuss those as well.

WHAT ARE CONNECTIONS?

The term that psychology uses for what we obtain from our connections—that is, interpersonal relationships—is "social support." Just as an Amazon search revealed our societal interest in friendship, a psychology search engine for 2000 to the present listed more than 60,000 entries for interpersonal relationships—books, research articles, dissertations, and collections of resources—reflecting psychologists' interest in this topic. There are two primary reasons for this interest. First, public health experts have conducted many longitudinal (long-term) studies of large groups of adults to pinpoint factors associated with lower mortality rates (fewer deaths). Those studies repeatedly found that having social connections was linked to longer life, even after other factors such as age and physical health were included in the analysis. The second reason for psychologists' interest is the other side of the coin: Studies of adults who did not have close personal ties documented that the risk of death from loneliness is similar to the risks from smoking and obesity.

WHAT ARE SOCIAL NETWORKS?

Psychologists think about connections through the concept of social networks. *Social networks* are the webs of people around you with whom you interact. Obviously, the term "social networks" encompasses a wide variety of possibilities. Your family is a social network, and your work colleagues are as well, as are your book club, your neighbors, your workout partners, your kids' friends, their parents, and so on. Social networks differ from one another, most obviously in size but also in other characteristics.

Density refers to how well your network members know each other. If you lived in a remote location with only a small number of people available for social interaction, your network would be completely dense because every member of it would know every other member. In contrast, if you had a network of friends from every place you've lived, none of whom know each other, you would have a low-density network.

Formality refers to whether your networks exist in an organizational structure, such as a workplace, a church or synagogue or mosque, a social organization, or a professional organization. Interactions between members of highly formal networks take place only within that formal structure. Interactions between members of less formal networks happen both within and outside the organizational structure. The reason formal organizations are important to networks is that an organization may have its own rules for how members relate to one another.

Another way networks differ is whether they are digital or face to face. Digital social networks are an important part of people's lives. These networks are so common that their use is known as "social networking." Digital networks provide solidarity, global connectivity, and personal support. Research suggests that when social networks encourage connection, they also encourage well-being; if they promote isolation or social comparison, they harm well-being (Clark et al., 2018).

To summarize, here is what we know about social networks:

- Social networks are webs of relationships among people that provide a range of positive benefits, such as emotional support and tangible support.
- Social networks differ in characteristics such as size, density, and formality.
- Digital social networks appear to be helpful if they increase connection but harmful if they increase isolation or social comparison.

WHAT IS SOCIAL SUPPORT?

How can social networks assist us in our recovery? They do so by providing social support. *Social support* is the benefits you receive from your social networks. Four types of social support have been identified. The first is emotional support. Social network members provide caring and companionship for one another. The second is instrumental support. If you are moving, for example, and members of your network come to help carry boxes and move furniture, they are providing instrumental support. The third is information support. Members of your network can help you solve problems by providing information and advice. The fourth is appraisal support. Social networks are a source of information that helps you evaluate yourself and your actions. Self-Assessment 8.1 helps you consider the strength of your own social network.

A study of 900 adults used the measure in Self-Assessment 8.1 to examine how participants' social networks affected their level of depression (Werner-Seidler et al., 2017). The researchers were interested in several aspects of participants' networks, including frequency of contact with family, frequency of contact with friends, and relationship quality—that is, whether they could confide in and rely on their family and friends. The frequency of participants' contact with their family networks had no impact on their depression, but participants who had family members they could confide in had lower levels of depression. Participants who had both more frequent contact with friendship networks and friends to confide in also had lower levels of depression. The authors concluded that the quality of relationships in social networks is more important to mental health than the frequency of contact.

Self-Assessment 8.1

How Strong Is Your Social Network?

In your journal or note-taking app, write down your responses to these questions using the options that appear below each question:

1. How often are you in contact with any members of your family, including visits, phone calls, letters, emails, or text messages?
   Nearly every day, 3–4 days a week, 1–2 days a week, 1–3 days a month, less than once a month, never
2. How often are you in contact with any of your friends, including visits, phone calls, letters, emails, or text messages?
   Nearly every day, 3–4 days a week, 1–2 days a week, 1–3 days a month, less than once a month, never
3. How many family members can you rely on?
   0, 1–2, 3–4, 5 or more
4. How many family members can you confide in?
   0, 1–2, 3–4, 5 or more
5. How many friends can you rely on?
   0, 1–2, 3–4, 5 or more
6. How many friends can you confide in?
   0, 1–2, 3–4, 5 or more

There is no exact method of scoring, but looking at your answers for the family items (Items 1, 3, and 4) and the friends items (Items 2, 5, and 6) together will give you an overall idea of the strength of your family and friendship networks. In the study behind this measure, lower depression was associated with having three or more friends to confide in, having three or more family members to confide in, and having contact with a network member more often than one to three times a month.

From "The Relationship Between Social Support Networks and Depression in the 2007 National Survey of Mental Health and Well-Being," by A. Werner-Seidler, M. H. Afzali, C. Chapman, M. Sunderland, and T. Slade, 2017, *Social Psychiatry and Psychiatric Epidemiology*, 52(12), Supplementary Materials (https://doi.org/10.1007/s00127-017-1440-7). Copyright 2017 by Springer Nature. Reprinted with permission.

WHAT IS PERCEIVED SOCIAL SUPPORT?

Psychologists interested in social support soon realized that some people have no networks at all, or only one or two friends. Yet some of these people feel very supported by their friends and are highly satisfied with their support. You may know someone with few close friends who is content with those friendships, or you may feel that way yourself. That is true because of *perceived social support*, which is the term used for how we experience the social support we receive regardless of the characteristics of our social networks, such as size or density. How we experience support can be very different from what appears available to us, which is why we can feel lonely in a crowd of people.

Two psychologists, Dan Russell and Carolyn Cutrona (1991), studied social support as it exists in dyadic (two-person) relationships and other contexts, and they outlined a model of social provisions. *Social provisions* are what we experience in social connection that is helpful to us—that is, what those connections provide. Self-Assessment 8.2 gives you an opportunity to explore the social provisions you receive from your support network.

According to Russell and Cutrona, we obtain six categories of provisions from our connections with other people. Some provisions fit better in certain types of relationships, and multiple categories of provisions can be gotten from the same person. Also, some provisions may be more or less important to us depending on where we are in the life cycle.

1. *Attachment* is an emotional bond that provides us with a sense of security.
2. *Social integration* is the sense of belonging to a group, small or large, of people with whom we share interests and enjoy similar activities.

Self-Assessment 8.2

How Strong Are Your Social Provisions?

The statements listed below describe the types of support provided by social connections. Think about your current relationships with friends, family members, coworkers, community members, and so on, and in your journal or note-taking app, indicate your agreement with each statement using this scale: 4 = *strongly agree*, 3 = *agree*, 2 = *disagree*, and 1 = *strongly disagree*.

1. There are people I can depend on to help me if I really need it.
2. I feel that I do not have close personal relationships with other people.
3. There is no one I can turn to for guidance in times of stress.
4. There are people who depend on me for help.
5. There are people who enjoy the same social activities I do.
6. Other people do not view me as competent.
7. I feel personally responsible for the well-being of another person.
8. I feel part of a group of people who share my attitudes and beliefs.
9. I do not think other people respect my skills and abilities.
10. If something went wrong, no one would come to my assistance.
11. I have close relationships that provide me with a sense of emotional security and well-being.
12. There is someone I could talk to about important decisions in my life.
13. I have relationships where my competence and skill are recognized.
14. There is no one who shares my interests and concerns.
15. There is no one who really relies on me for their well-being.
16. There is a trustworthy person I could turn to for advice if I were having problems.
17. I feel a strong emotional bond with at least one other person.
18. There is no one I can depend on for aid if I really need it.
19. There is no one I feel comfortable talking about problems with.
20. There are people who admire my talents and abilities.
21. I lack a feeling of intimacy with another person.

(continues)

Self-Assessment 8.2 (*Continued*)

22. There is no one who likes to do the things I do.
23. There are people I can count on in an emergency.
24. No one needs me to care for them.

Your scores on this test indicate how strong your social provisions are in each category. Begin by "reversing" the scoring for items that have an asterisk in the list below: If you wrote a 1, change it to a 4; if you wrote a 2, change it to a 3; if you wrote a 3, change it to a 2; and if you wrote a 4, change it to a 1. Then add up your scores for each category.

- Attachment: Items 2,* 11, 17, and 21*
- Social integration: Items 5, 8, 14,* and 22*
- Reassurance of worth: Items 6,* 9,* 13, and 20
- Reliable alliance: Items 1, 10,* 18,* and 23
- Guidance: Items 3,* 12, 16, and 19*
- Opportunity for nurturance: Items 4, 7, 15,* and 24*

In your journal or note-taking app, write down the social provision category with the lowest score; this is the area in which you receive the least support. What specific things can you do to increase the support you receive? Then select the social provision category with the highest score; this is the area in which you receive the strongest support. How do you find that the support you receive in that area helps you? Then go back and review your social network scores from Self-Assessment 8.1 and see how they fit or do not fit with your social provisions scores. Remember that having a social network does not necessarily mean you are receiving support. You may find that more frequent contact or closer relationships can give you the support you need.

3. *Reassurance of worth* is felt when our skills, abilities, or competencies are recognized and valued by others.
4. *Reliable alliance* is a friend or other social connection who can be relied on for tangible assistance, such as money or equipment, or help with a problem.
5. *Guidance* is advice, support, problem solving, listening, and other help with life challenges.
6. *Opportunity for nurturance* is the knowledge that another person relies on us, and that we benefit from being responsible in some way for the well-being of another person.

As with social network research, studies of social provisions have demonstrated that there are mental health and physical health benefits from feeling supported by others. Perceiving support from other people leads to lower depression, more positive emotions, and enhanced well-being (a review by Wang et al., 2018, provides more information about this research). The possibility that some social provisions are better suited to certain times or circumstances in a person's life led psychologists to try to "match" provisions to life circumstances. For example, if a stressful event is controllable—that is, if it can be prevented or its consequences reduced—the optimal social provisions are guidance, especially information, and reassurance of worth. If the stressful event is uncontrollable—that is, not preventable—then the optimal provision is social integration. If the stressful event is a loss of resources, then reliable alliance is a good match. If the loss is in relationships, such as bereavement, then attachment is important. In any life event, opportunity for nurturance is helpful because people who have experienced stressful circumstances become better positioned to help others in similar circumstances.

Differences in circumstances and individuals affect the provision and perception of support. For example, as I was writing this book, the COVID-19 pandemic was altering the lives of millions. The enforced isolation of social distancing and community lockdowns has been linked to increased depression and anxiety. An online study of almost 3,000 adults during the pandemic revealed that 40% had a medium or high level of depression and that 20% had a medium or high level of anxiety (Mazza et al., 2020). For many people, the enforced isolation affected the provision or perception of support and may have contributed to mental health problems.

To summarize, here is what we know about social support:

- *Social support* is the benefits you receive from your networks.
- Traditional (face-to-face) social networks are associated with improved mental health among members who have frequent contact and close personal ties with other members.
- Perceptions of support from others are an essential part of social support. People may feel completely supported even with a small network consisting of a few friends or family members.
- Social support involves receiving certain benefits from other people, called "social provisions." Those benefits are attachment, social integration, reassurance of worth, reliable alliance, guidance, and opportunity for nurturance.
- Some social provisions best match specific life events. But differences among people and the circumstances of their lives also influence how well a provision matches their need for support.

WHAT ROLE DOES SOCIAL SUPPORT PLAY AFTER TRAUMA?

When psychologists think about social support during and after trauma, there are two aspects of attachment theory they find helpful: "safe haven" and "secure base." Remember, "attachment" is an emotional bond, and attachment theory describes how people develop those bonds. Attachment theory starts with infants being born ready for social interaction with concerned and consistent caregivers, usually the mother. Infants who experience caring and consistent responses from a caregiver develop a secure attachment. In the next year, the young child engages in exploration of the world. The same caring parent now provides a base from which the child can leave and to which he or she can return. Secure attachment, then, results in nurturance, or safe haven, and in autonomy, or secure base.

What does social support after trauma look like in practice? As adult survivors, our trauma is in the past. Yet we experience intrusions of that history in our present. For example, hearing about the abuse of a child we know would likely be a trigger to memories of our own, and perhaps panic and nightmares. We need a support person who can listen carefully (safe haven) to our experiences and accept our emotions without being overwhelmed by them. And we need a support person to help us cope (secure base), perhaps by reminding us to journal our feelings or to go back and reread journaling we have done in the past.

Sometimes we are in a relationship in which we feel that the support we are receiving isn't really supportive. Why might that be the case? Because conversation that seems to be meant to be supportive can actually be the reverse. Emotional support provided by others can be positive, neutral, or negative. One might think that after a trauma, positive support would be the best response, negative support the worst, and neutral support somewhere in between. However, the findings of a study of support after a traumatic event did not agree with this intuitive perspective (Pruitt & Zoellner, 2008). Two psychologists asked 100 adults to view a distressing video of a violent trauma and to respond as if they were the victim. Participants then received a communication that provided positive, negative, or neutral emotional support; these communications were modeled on actual interactions (you may recognize these statements):

- Positive support consisted of validating the participant's response, avoiding blaming the participant, sharing a similar past experience, promoting trust, avoiding stigmatization, giving positive emotional support, and making offers of aid. An example statement was "That sounds really serious. I am so glad you are safe."

- Negative support consisted of invalidating the participant's response, shutting down the conversation, blaming the participant, taking over the focus of the conversation, giving negative emotional support, and attempting to control the participant's responses. An example statement was "Calm down; it wasn't that serious. You're alive, aren't you? I don't know why you want to talk about it."

- Neutral support consisted of providing a simple acknowledgment, discussing unrelated events, blaming a third party, avoiding emotional expression, and not offering help. An example statement was "I am sure that happens to lots of people."

In this study, negative social support was associated with higher levels of depression than positive social support. However, participants who received neutral support reported more symptoms typical of posttraumatic stress disorder, such as intrusive thoughts, and a more negative view of the traumatic event. The authors of this study concluded that for trauma survivors, a neutral response indicates a rejection of their emotional state and feels like an invalidation of their need for support.

To summarize, here is what we know about social support after a trauma:

- Support after trauma is best when it reinforces nurturance (safe haven) and allows autonomy (secure base).
- Social support helps trauma survivors when it is positive and hurts them when it is neutral or negative.

WHAT ABOUT SOCIAL SUPPORT AFTER CHILDHOOD SEXUAL ABUSE?

Adults who experienced childhood sexual abuse have two specific problems with social support that other trauma survivors don't have. The first problem is that abuse survivors receive less social support: They report having smaller networks, being less satisfied with the social support they do receive, and seeing their interpersonal connections as less supportive (Vranceanu et al., 2007). The second problem is that abuse survivors require more social support: They experience more distress and disorders of mood and thought as after-effects of their abuse experience, and they have greater exposure to adversities (see Chapter 1).

This trajectory toward receiving less and requiring more social support begins in childhood. As victims of abuse, children see the world as a dangerous place and anticipate further harm. These thoughts lead them to withdraw from potential sources of support that they do not see as safe. Negative attachment styles develop and are then reinforced by experiences of revictimization. As adults, survivors expect that resources provided by family or friends will not be sufficient to match their intense reactions of fear, anger, and avoidance. We know that some of our family and friends simply cannot "hold" the emotions and memories we experience.

Catherine Townsend, who has worked with the organization Darkness to Light, summarized research about disclosing childhood sexual abuse (Townsend et al., 2016). This research has established that children rarely disclose their abuse. Even when there is objective evidence, such as a medical report, up to 43% of children still are not willing to disclose. Why do children not tell? Some may have been threatened by the perpetrator, some may fear being disbelieved or blamed, some may worry about the consequences for the perpetrator. For most, that silence carries into adulthood. It may take a counseling relationship or a supportive friendship to increase their confidence sufficiently to disclose their abuse.

In a chapter on connection, it seems logical to turn to the biological family of origin. Unfortunately, because virtually all childhood sexual abuse occurs within families or by adults who are trusted by families, the family may not be a source of connection and social support. Although there are many differences among families in which childhood sexual abuse occurs, three characteristics contribute to a family environment in which abuse is not dealt with effectively.

The first characteristic is a family culture of secrecy or gender-related power imbalance. A strictly isolated environment in which the family keeps everything "inside the family" is common in abusive situations; the isolation may be physical or social. Many families do not report the abuse to anyone outside the family because it "isn't anyone else's business." Another cultural characteristic common in abusive families is subservience of female members to male members. Many families with a male-dominant culture do not engage in or tolerate abuse. But virtually all abuse within families is done by male members to female members, and that subservience may place girls and women at risk for abuse (Finkelhor, 1984).

A second characteristic that prevents families from dealing with abuse effectively is problematic unspoken "rules" that govern communication within the family. Some families have an unspoken rule that there will be no upsetting the father or mother. Another unspoken rule is that nothing is said to a person who is the actual subject of a communication. As an example, a teenager is told by her aunt that her mother is upset with something the teenager did, but the mother will not talk to the teenager directly. Another example is a family in which one person is the single communicator. This family's communication map looks like a wagon wheel with spokes going out from the hub. All family members tell everything to the dominant parent, who then passes the information along as or when they choose. When a family member sees or experiences abuse, no one will speak up except the hub person.

A third characteristic of families in which abuse is tolerated or ignored is enmeshment. *Enmeshment* occurs when family members have no boundaries or unclear boundaries; *boundaries* separate us from "not us" (that is, other people) in emotions, thoughts, and physical limits. In enmeshed families, it is difficult or not possible to separate the emotional life of one person from the emotional life of another. For example, a teenage daughter becomes anxious and depressed by school. Her mother then becomes anxious and depressed and becomes overinvolved in her daughter's life trying to "help" her. However, the mother is really responding from and trying to manage her own emotions, not her daughter's. The mother's overinvolvement prevents the daughter from becoming developmentally independent and may lead to a worsening of the daughter's experience. Abuse occurs more often and is covered up in families with enmeshment.

If abuse is disclosed, these characteristics of the family environment play a role in the dysfunction caused by the disclosure. If a family keeps secrets, no one will report the abuse, and they may actually deny the abuse is occurring; disclosure of the abuse incinerates that strategy, and great anxiety and confusion follow.

If a family has unspoken communication rules, the disclosure is likely to violate all of those rules. Adult survivors who disclose abuse face abandonment by the family or are encouraged by the family to ignore or minimize the abuse.

To summarize, here is what we know about social support after childhood sexual abuse:

- Child abuse results in adult trauma symptoms and in attachment styles that do not lead easily to finding social support.
- The benefits of connection for abuse survivors are well established.

HOW CAN YOUR CONNECTIONS HELP YOUR RECOVERY JOURNEY?

Compassion is a process that contains four elements: becoming aware of the suffering, being moved emotionally by the suffering, forming the intention to reduce the suffering, and taking action to reduce the suffering. Compassion can flow in three directions: (a) We feel compassion for other people, (b) we feel compassion coming to us from others, and (c) we direct compassion toward ourselves.

Self-compassion is a key to connection. Self-compassion was discussed in Chapter 3; if you have not read that chapter yet, here is a summary: Self-compassion has three parts (Neff, 2011). The first is self-kindness, which is being kind and understanding toward ourselves, rather than being harshly critical or judgmental. Some of us think that being self-critical is more likely to motivate us toward changes in behavior, but that is not true; it's more likely to promote shame than motivation. The second part of self-compassion is common humanity. We recognize that all of us have defects and all of us experience adversity; therefore, we do not need to feel shame when we fail or feel inadequate. The third part of self-compassion is mindfulness, or holding our experiences in a balanced way. Too often we are carried away by our own pain, or the opposite, we ignore our pain and pretend even to ourselves that we are "just fine." Mindfulness is the balanced awareness of our feelings and experiences.

It is important to keep in mind that not all of your connections have the capacity to support you as a survivor in the ways you need most urgently. But they still have important roles to play in your recovery. Perhaps they can go with you on a hike or to a concert. Any type of connection will provide you with benefits. One thing the pandemic has taught us is how much we appreciate and look forward to interactions with people that are routine, such as making conversation about the weather with a person you see in the elevator at work.

You will be better able to build and nurture your connections if you can maintain a positive view of the self, build your self-acceptance, and take a proactive approach to the world. A positive view of the self increases our motivation and confidence in forming connections. Self-acceptance and self-compassion are necessary to reduce our barriers of shame and avoidance. Finally, when we take a proactive approach to the world and stop waiting for something to happen to us, we instead go out and make things happen. It is not "silly" to need help in finding and making friends who will support you in your journey. The Resources section lists books and handbooks that will be helpful to you.

RESOURCES

Digital Resources

- *Child Sexual Abuse Disclosure: What Practitioners Need to Know* is a 2016 report by Catherine Townsend published by Darkness to Light, a nonprofit dedicated to preventing child sexual abuse (available at https://www.d2l.org/wp-content/uploads/2020/01/Child-Sexual-Abuse-Disclosure-Statistics-and-Literature-Review.pdf). Although the report was written for counselors, it covers many topics important to the issue of disclosure.

- The Crimes Against Children Research Center website (https://www.unh.edu/ccrc) makes available research studies about child victimization and other relevant topics such as sex trafficking, internet victimization, prevention, and adverse childhood experiences.

Print Resources

- *Here to Make Friends: How to Make Friends as an Adult*, by Hope Kelaher (Ulysses Press, 2020). The author is a social worker who specializes in helping clients build connections. This book explores friendship and tackles difficult steps such as finding friends and "putting yourself out there." There are exercises in each chapter to increase self-knowledge.
- *Love 2.0: Finding Happiness and Health in Moments of Connection*, by Barbara Fredrickson (Penguin Group, 2013). The author is the psychologist responsible for the broaden and build model of positive emotions discussed in Chapter 4. In this book, she takes what she has learned about positive emotions and connections to present a view of love that is different from traditional views.
- *The Courage to Heal*, by Ellen Bass and Laura Davis (Harper-Collins, 2008). This book was the original guide for women survivors of childhood sexual abuse. It presents basic and practical information on healing, with an emphasis on finding support. There are also stories from 17 women about their recovery journey.

- *The Sexual Healing Journey: A Guide for Survivors of Sexual Abuse*, by Wendy Maltz (William Morrow, 2012). Experiencing sexual abuse as a child can disrupt adult sexuality. The abuse affects how we feel about our bodies, about expressing ourselves sexually, and about experiencing pleasure and intimacy with another. This book is directed specifically to sexual healing on the emotional and physical levels.

CHAPTER 9

FORGIVENESS

Recovery Milestones

This chapter will help you

1. **understand** the true meaning of forgiveness,
2. **recognize** barriers to forgiveness,
3. **learn** how forgiveness can contribute to your well-being, and
4. **identify** the steps or phases of forgiveness.

This may be the last chapter you are reading in this book. If that is not the case, then perhaps you opened to this page with a sigh or an eyeroll. I remember when I first talked with a pastor about my childhood. After I had explained, briefly, what my experiences were, he paused. Then he thought. Then he said, "Well, of course you will want to forgive your father." *Of course*. There was no "of course" about it. I think everyone who is a survivor has endured from someone, well-meaning or not, a conversation about the supposed benefits of forgiveness, or the religious necessity, or how well it worked for someone else. And that conversation becomes a heavy burden.

I do not want this chapter to be that burden for you. I do want to be sure you accurately understand forgiveness because there are so many misunderstandings about it. I want you to know what benefits forgiveness has been shown to bring to people. Because the world's religions have much to say about forgiveness, people believe it pertains only to religion. However, psychology has contributed much that is useful to our understanding of forgiveness.

WHAT IS FORGIVENESS?

The term psychologists use for actions that harm a person is "transgressions." If those transgressions are interpersonal, they are committed by an "offender" against a "victim." Transgressions intentionally caused by an offender are experienced as deeply wounding by the victim. Schultz et al. (2010) interviewed 150 adults who volunteered to discuss a time they had been significantly wronged by another person. The transgressions ranged from physical harm, infidelity, and assault to slander and betrayal. Ratings of distress showed that even transgressions that might sound less significant, such as slander, were very disturbing to the victims.

Additionally, transgressions do not have to be caused by the deliberate actions of others to create a sense of being personally wounded. Psychologists who studied survivors of a devastating tsunami showed that a common response by victims was to blame someone (Roxberg et al., 2010). Examples of people they blamed were those who should have triggered an earlier warning, first responders, the government, and even other victims. Transgressions can also be caused by a stranger who remains unknown to the victim, or by a group of people, or by someone whose actions were unintentional or even unrecognized.

Misunderstandings of Forgiveness

Although psychologists may emphasize different parts of forgiveness, such as motivation or emotion, there is definite agreement on concepts that are *not* the same as forgiveness. Many of these concepts have been confused with forgiveness, which makes it essential to understand them accurately.

People who learn of a transgression sometimes try to encourage the victim to forgive in ways that reflect a misunderstanding of forgiveness. Their responses to the transgression might include the following:

- *Condoning:* Condoning minimizes the impact of the transgression on the victim. It also redefines the transgression as acceptable behavior. An example of a condoning response to the transgression is "It wasn't that big a deal." A condoning response tells the victim that their anger is not reasonable.

- *Justifying:* Justifying balances the transgression against the supposed reasons behind it. An example of a justifying response to the transgression is "She didn't mean it." Another example is "He was just having a bad day." Justifying tells the victim that the transgression was not as bad as the victim perceives it because there were reasons that it happened.

- *Telling the victim to forget:* Forgetting is frequently confused with forgiveness. Have you ever heard "forgive and forget"? But some transgressions do not get forgotten, even if they are forgiven. True forgiveness does not deny the reality of the harm, but it changes the victim's response to it. Even if forgiveness has taken place, forgetting may not.

- *Recommending reconciliation:* Reconciliation is a process that restores and renews a broken relationship. Reconciliation reestablishes trust and caring between two persons. But it is a two-person process. There are necessary actions on the part of the offender. A victim can forgive an offender without being reconciled to him or her. That is important to keep in mind, because it might not be safe to pursue a reconciliation, or the offender might be dead or out of reach.

In addition, victims may be unwilling to face the need to forgive because of the following misunderstandings:

- *Fear of confronting the offender:* Being afraid to confront the offender prompts a short-circuiting of the process. If we are afraid to say what we feel or think, we jump ahead and decide that we have forgiven the offense. But denying the reality of the offender's actions does not allow us to actually reach forgiveness and, in fact, will prevent it.
- *Fear of acknowledging our own anger:* Some of us have been told that anger is not an acceptable response to being harmed. Others of us fear that if we acknowledge our anger, we will lose control of our feelings and be overwhelmed by them. Acknowledging anger and giving it a rightful place in our experience is a necessary part of forgiveness.
- *Belief that forgiveness requires an apology:* Forgiveness is a process that occurs within one person, the victim. To require an apology before we decide to forgive lets the responsibility for forgiveness reside in the offender, rather than ourselves.
- *Belief that forgiveness means we are weak:* Forgiveness is an act of strength, not of weakness. It is easy to give in to our feelings in response to a transgression and to ruminate—that is, think repetitively and negatively—about our pain. It is hard to have pain and suffering and still decide to forgive.

Forgiveness Is Change

Forgiveness is change in several areas of our being. First, it is *motivational:* We give up motives of revenge toward the offender, and we adopt more conciliatory (peacemaking) or neutral motives. Forgiveness is *decisional:* We decide to change negative intentions to neutral or even positive intentions. Forgiveness is *emotional:* We reduce our feelings of rage and bitterness and increase our feelings of goodwill. In forgiveness, we gradually replace negative thoughts, feelings, and actions with neutral or positive thoughts, feelings, and actions. The negatives include anger, intent to carry out revenge, bitterness, rumination about the offense, and fear of being harmed again in the future. The positives include acting in a kindly way toward the offender and having empathy for him or her. Self-Assessment 9.1 gives you an opportunity to examine your motives in response to a transgression against you.

To summarize, here is what we know about forgiveness:

- Forgiveness is a response to being wounded or harmed by another person or force or group, called a "transgression."
- Forgiveness is a process that begins with an accurate acceptance of the transgression and its consequences in the victim's life.
- Forgiveness is not the same as condoning, justifying, ignoring, avoiding, delaying, or forgetting the transgression.
- Forgiveness is a process that belongs only to the victim; it does not require an apology or reconciliation.

WHAT ARE INFLUENCES ON FORGIVENESS?

Under what circumstances do people forgive offenders? Many studies have been completed on the influence of various factors on forgiveness. A group of psychologists pulled together the results from a large number of studies in a meta-analysis that considered three types of influences on forgiveness: thoughts (cognitions) of the victim, emotions of the victim, and aspects of the situation (contextual influences; Fehr et al., 2010). Here is a summary of what they found:

- *The victim's thoughts:* When victims believed that the transgression was severe or that the offender intentionally caused

Self-Assessment 9.1

Forgiveness Motivations

Think about a specific transgression against you by a single offender—the person who hurt you. How do you feel about that person right now? In your journal or note-taking app, write down how accurately each statement describes how you feel using this scale: 1 = *strongly disagree*, 2 = *disagree*, 3 = *neutral*, 4 = *agree*, and 5 = *strongly agree*.

1. I will make him/her pay.
2. I am trying to keep as much distance between us as possible.
3. Even though his/her actions hurt me, I have goodwill for him/her.
4. I wish that something bad would happen to him/her.
5. I am living as if he/she doesn't exist, or isn't around.
6. I want to bury the hatchet and move forward with our relationship.
7. I don't trust him/her.
8. Despite what he/she did, I want us to have a positive relationship again.
9. I want him/her to get what he/she deserves.
10. I am finding it difficult to act warmly toward him/her.
11. I am avoiding him/her.
12. Although he/she hurt me, I am putting the hurts aside so we can resume our relationship.
13. I am going to get even.
14. I have given up my hurt and resentment.
15. I cut off the relationship with him/her.
16. I have released my anger so I can work on restoring our relationship to health.
17. I want to see him/her hurt and miserable.
18. I withdraw from him/her.

Calculate your average scores in the following categories:

- Avoidance motivations: Items 2, 5, 7, 10, 11, 15 and 18 (add your scores for these items and divide by 7)
- Revenge motivations: Items 1, 4, 9, 13 and 17 (add your scores for these items and divide by 5)

Self-Assessment 9.1 (*Continued*)

- Benevolence (willingness to forgive) motivations: Items 3, 6, 8, 12, 14 and 16 (add your scores for these items and divide by 6).

In your journal or note-taking app, describe how your scores present a picture of your motivations toward a person who hurt you. Which motivations are the strongest for you? Which are the weakest? What surprised you about your scores?

Adapted from "Interpersonal Forgiving in Close Relationships: II. Theoretical Elaboration and Measurement," by M. E. McCullough, K. C. Rachal, S. J. Sandage, E. L. Worthington, Jr., S. W. Brown, and T. L. Hight, 1998, *Journal of Personality and Social Psychology, 75*(6), p. 1603 (https://doi.org/10.1037/0022-3514.75.6.1586). Copyright 1998 by the American Psychological Association; and "Transgression-Related Motivational Dispositions: Personality Substrates of Forgiveness and Their Links to the Big Five," by M. E. McCullough and W. T. Hoyt, 2002, *Personality and Social Psychology Bulletin, 28*(11), p. 1572 (https://doi.org/10.1177/014616702237583). Copyright 2002 by SAGE. Adapted with permission.

---

them harm, they were less likely to forgive. When victims ruminated over the transgression, they were less likely to forgive. However, receiving a sincere apology from the offender increased the likelihood of forgiveness. Other factors that increased forgiveness were the victims' ability to understand the perspective of the offender and their tendency to typically or often forgive transgressions.

- *The victim's feelings:* When victims experienced many negative feelings, such as depression or anger, they were less likely to forgive. If victims normally experienced negative emotions strongly, they were also less likely to forgive. If victims tended to be angry in response to many situations in life, then forgiveness of a transgression was less likely. However, if victims had empathy for the offender, or a high level of self-esteem, forgiveness was more likely to occur.

- *Aspects of the situation:* If victims were in a close relationship with the offender, if that relationship was satisfying, and if there was a high degree of commitment in the relationship, they were more likely to forgive. However, if victims believed that the transgression would recur or that the offender would act in a similar way in the future, they were less likely to forgive. Age, gender, and time since the offense did not affect the likelihood of forgiveness.

To summarize, here is what we know about influences on forgiveness:

- If transgressions are more severe, are seen as intentional, or caused the victim a great amount of pain, then forgiveness is less likely.
- If the victim and the offender are in a relationship of some type, such as family or romantic, then forgiveness is more likely if that relationship is a committed one and has been satisfying in the past.
- Being male or female, older or younger, or closer to or farther away from the transgression in time does not seem to affect forgiveness.

HOW DOES FORGIVENESS WORK IN THE BRAIN?

You might be thinking of forgiveness as a set of events that do not have any basis in the biochemical workings of your body. But that viewpoint would be wrong. Psychologists have recently been studying how forgiveness takes place in the brain. Three neuroscientists examined the results of 15 published studies about forgiveness that presented neuroimaging results (Fourie et al., 2020). *Neuroimaging* is the use of advanced computerized technologies to provide pictures of regions or areas of the brain; those regions "light up" to show brain activity during specific tasks or behaviors. These researchers considered forgiveness to be three different but interacting processes. The first process is cognitive control. *Cognitive control* means that the victim overcomes strong negative emotions, reduces ruminative thoughts, reduces the impulse to get revenge, and tries to have empathy for the offender. These cognitive tasks—regulating emotions, reducing cognitive conflict, and countering response tendencies—occur in specific areas of the brain. Those areas light up in brain images when people are engaged in those tasks.

The second process is perspective taking. *Perspective taking* occurs when the victim suspends, or pauses, their own point of view in order to understand the point of view of the offender. One way to achieve that is mentalizing: *Mentalizing* is using your thoughts to "think about your thinking." Perspective taking and mentalizing occur in specific areas of the brain different from areas associated with cognitive control. Again, these areas light up when people are engaging in those tasks.

The third process is social valuation. *Social valuation* happens when the victim engages in a cost–benefit analysis, weighing various influences on the decision to forgive or not to forgive the offender. We know that situational factors influence the social valuation of forgiveness: Examples of these factors are whether an apology is given, the severity of the transgression, and the relationship (if any) within which the transgression occurred. There may also be moral judgments about the rightness or wrongness of the action. These tasks—cost–benefit analysis, relational value, and moral judgments—occur in specific areas of the brain different from the areas associated with cognitive control and perspective taking. And again, those areas light up during the relevant tasks.

What does this research tell us? First, forgiveness is a complex response that takes place in multiple areas of our brain, each of them in control of some but not all aspects of that response. Second, the sheer amount of brain activity stimulated by forgiveness processes suggests that it is an important part of our humanity. The degree to which we are social beings reflects the importance of forgiveness to maintaining those social connections. Third, forgiveness is not only a matter of psychological features, such as emotions or actions; rather, it has definite biological components as well.

WHAT ARE THE BARRIERS TO FORGIVENESS?

We know that we, and many others, find it hard to forgive some transgressions. The transgression may have been so painful, or betrayed shared norms and values so deeply, that forgiveness seems impossible. There may be reasons why withholding forgiveness seems a better choice. By doing so, we may hold on to a "right" to compensation or reparation, feel we are morally superior, or believe that not forgiving allows us to have more power in the relationship.

Three psychologists decided that it was important to study barriers to forgiveness (Pearce et al., 2018). They proposed two primary types of barriers:

1. *Reactive barriers:* Reactive barriers are about the present: the event, the hurt it caused, and the pain being suffered. For example, one reactive barrier is the perceived severity of the transgression. Some transgressions are a deep betrayal of the trust the victim had in the offender. If trust is destroyed by the transgression, forgiveness is harder. Another reactive barrier involves the type of transgression. If the transgression is seen by the victim as morally reprehensible, then the victim may

feel disgust, contempt, and rage toward the offender and be unable to forgive.

2. *Active barriers:* Active barriers are about the future, the "what is next" after the transgression. If the victim does not forgive the offender, then the victim is sending the offender a message that the transgression was not acceptable and that the offender will not get away with it. If the victim and offender are in a relationship, then not forgiving is a way of punishing the offender for the transgression. The victim may also believe that not forgiving the offender will increase the offender's sense of guilt, thereby protecting the victim from future transgressions.

Self-Assessment 9.2 gives you a way to understand your own barriers to forgiveness.

WHAT ARE THE BENEFITS OF FORGIVENESS?

It is reasonable to ask what happens when we do forgive and, in contrast, what happens when we do not forgive. Psychologists have been interested in both questions and are beginning to find solid answers.

Mental Health and Physical Health Benefits

Because forgiveness occurs in the context of a transgression, forgiveness serves as a type of coping strategy for facing the difficulties of the transgression. Three psychologists used this perspective in a study on forgiveness in which they asked 320 adults about their mental health and their forgiveness (Maltby et al., 2004). People who did not forgive experienced more anger, anxiety, depression, and perceived stress and less life satisfaction. In contrast, people

Self-Assessment 9.2

Barriers to Forgiveness

The statements listed below have to do with specific reasons you have not forgiven a person who hurt you. There are no right or wrong answers; everyone has different reasons for not forgiving. In your journal or note-taking app, write down the number that indicates how accurately each statement describes your reason for not forgiving that person using this scale: 1 = *strongly disagree*, 2 = *disagree*, 3 = *neutral or not sure*, 4 = *agree*, or 5 = *strongly agree*.

I have not forgiven them because . . .

1. Forgiving that person might make me lose face in front of others.
2. I do not want the other person to think I can't or won't stand up for myself.
3. What they did was too wrong or reprehensible to forgive.
4. What they did permanently severed all trust between us.
5. If I forgave, I would no longer be able to make them feel guilty or bad about what they did.
6. It might make others see me as weak or foolish.
7. I am too disgusted by what they did.
8. Our relationship has been irreparably damaged by what they did.
9. I want to get back at them for what they did.
10. I want to be able to use what they did against them in the future.
11. I have too strong a stance against what they did.
12. The event is still too distressing to me.
13. I do not want other people to think I would let someone treat me like that.
14. I do not want my willingness to forgive to be seen as a weakness to be exploited or manipulated.
15. I could never forgive someone who could do something like that.
16. Some things just cannot and should not be forgiven.
17. I do not want them and/or other people to see me as a pushover.
18. By not forgiving them, I am punishing them for what they did.
19. My opinion of them has changed too much as a result of how they acted.

Self-Assessment 9.2 (*Continued*)

20. I continue to feel anger and resentment when I think about the other person and/or what they did.

Calculate your scores adding up the responses in the following categories:

- Reactive barriers: Items 3, 4, 7, 8, 11, 12, 15, 16, 19, and 20
- Active barriers: Items 1, 2, 5, 6, 9, 10, 13, 14, 17, and 18.

This self-assessment can help you better understand your own barriers to forgiveness. In research with this scale, participants were more likely to score higher in active barriers than reactive barriers. Which barrier is most important to you right now? What aspects of the transgression do you see as creating that barrier?

From "The Barriers to Forgiveness Scale: A Measure of Active and Reactive Reasons for Withholding Forgiveness," by H. Pearce, P. Strelan, and N. R. Burns, 2018, *Personality and Individual Differences, 134*, p. 340 (https://doi.org/10.1016/j.paid.2018.06.042). Copyright 2018 by Elsevier. Reprinted with permission.

who did forgive experienced less stress, more positive emotions, and more life satisfaction. This conclusion is supported by other research findings that unforgiveness leads to negative emotions, less well-being, anger, anxiety, and life dissatisfaction (see Griffin et al., 2015, for a review). Forgiveness is linked to lower levels of negative emotions, such as depression, and higher levels of positive emotions, such as life satisfaction.

A single act of forgiveness, for an event of great importance, has significant benefits. But it is equally valuable to consider how repeated acts of forgiveness work for people who have experienced many offenses or transgressions over time. Four psychologists who examined lifetime stress histories along with forgiveness and mental health made two interesting findings (Toussaint et al., 2016). First, people who tended to forgive others more often experienced better mental health. Second, people with severe stress who forgave offenders had fewer mental health problems than those who were not as forgiving.

Psychologists have also considered whether forgiveness influences physical health. A meta-analysis of 128 published studies found that overall, forgiveness of others was associated with better physical health, measured in many different ways (Lee & Enright, 2019). This benefit was not affected by other influences on physical health, such as age, gender, race, education, and employment. In other words, forgiveness was associated with better physical health for adults of all ages, races, education levels, and employment contexts.

Even beyond physical health, research has shown that forgiveness is related to mortality (deaths). A study of more than 1,000 adults examined several types of forgiveness, including conditional forgiveness (Toussaint et al., 2012). In *conditional forgiveness*, the victim requires a "condition" before forgiving the offender—for example, an apology or some type of restitution. Because the offender must also participate, this is not true forgiveness. The authors found that conditional forgiveness was associated with higher mortality.

Spiritual Transformation and Posttraumatic Growth

Survivors of childhood sexual abuse have experienced a transgression like no other. It has been termed "soul murder," and that is why forgiveness requires strength. Recall from Chapter 7 that spiritual transformation can be either positive or negative, and each type has consequences for mental health. Jessica Schultz, a psychologist who studied forgiveness, investigated whether forgiveness of a significant interpersonal transgression might affect spiritual transformation and, in turn, well-being.

In Schultz's (2011) study, 146 men and women who were ethnically diverse (more than half self-identified as a person of color) described the impact of a harmful interpersonal transgression, their forgiveness of the offender, and their spiritual gain or decline. Among these participants, greater distress from the transgression was associated with less forgiveness, and less forgiveness led to spiritual decline. But a spiritual gain was linked to the outcome of posttraumatic growth. Recall from Chapter 3 that posttraumatic growth happens as the person experiences enduring benefits after a trauma beyond a return to the way they were before it. These benefits included improved relationships, new directions in life, a stronger appreciation of life, a sense of being stronger and more capable, and spiritual changes.

In another study of forgiveness and posttraumatic growth, 285 adults who lost an intimate partner, spouse, or close friend in the 2007 mass shooting at Virginia Tech were surveyed twice: 3 to 4 months and 1 year after the shooting (Wusik et al., 2015). Distress, forgiveness of the shooter, and posttraumatic growth were measured at both time points. High levels of distress 3 to 4 months after the shooting led to forgiveness, which in turn led to posttraumatic growth 1 year later. This finding indicates that people can achieve forgiveness in a way that will give them greater benefits in the future.

To summarize, here is what we know about the benefits of forgiveness:

- Forgiveness is related to better mental health, such as lower anxiety, depression, and anger, and to greater life satisfaction and emotional well-being.
- Forgiveness also has physical health benefits, including reduced mortality.
- Forgiveness is associated with positive spiritual transformation and with posttraumatic growth.

WHAT ABOUT FORGIVENESS AFTER CHILDHOOD SEXUAL ABUSE?

I wish I could present you with research findings specific to forgiveness after childhood sexual abuse, but unfortunately little research has been conducted on this important topic. That makes sense to me because it is a challenging topic and would be hard to study. But research has been done on a type of forgiveness not yet considered in this chapter: self-forgiveness. Do you wake up with self-loathing? Do some memories lead to so much shame that you avoid them in any way? If so, self-forgiveness is important for you. *Self-forgiveness* is forgiveness of oneself, and it enables self-compassion and self-acceptance instead of self-hatred and shame.

A survey of 520 adults who had been sexually abused as children examined their forgiveness of themselves and their life satisfaction (Morton et al., 2019). People who had forgiven themselves reported greater life satisfaction. Self-forgiveness also decreased the anger and hostility they directed at the self. It may be that self-forgiveness allows survivors to hold negative emotions lightly, with mindfulness, rather than being overwhelmed by them.

A study of 79 college students who experienced sexual abuse as a child focused on their current experience of counterproductive hostility in their lives (Snyder & Heinze, 2005). Participants provided information on their abuse experience and levels of hostility and the degree to which they forgave the offender and themselves. For these participants, forgiving themselves reduced anger and hostility in their lives, but forgiving the perpetrator did not. The researchers believed that self-forgiveness allowed the victims to detach or separate from the debilitating and powerful hold of the abuse trauma.

The notion of self-hatred and shame in contrast to self-forgiveness was also considered in an intervention (treatment) study (Ha et al., 2019). Sixteen students who had been sexually abused as children participated in four sessions of a forgiveness writing intervention in which they wrote about their abuse, including emotions they experienced, forgiveness they had achieved, and meaning they had developed. They were compared to another group of 16 students who had experienced abuse but did not receive the writing intervention. The students who completed the intervention had less shame, improved depression, and greater posttraumatic growth. The authors of this study believed that the self-focus of the writing intervention allowed the participants to reprocess their trauma and reduce their shame and self-criticism, thereby increasing their self-forgiveness.

To summarize, here is what we know about forgiveness after childhood sexual abuse:

- Adult survivors who forgive themselves typically have greater emotional well-being, with less depression, anger, and anxiety.
- Self-forgiveness reduces the experience of shame, leading to increased life satisfaction.

HOW DO WE FORGIVE?

After a serious transgression, we do not simply "decide" to forgive. Rather, there is a process. We are indebted to Robert Enright, a psychologist who has spent his life understanding how people forgive. He outlined a four-step model of forgiveness: uncovering, decision, work, and deepening (Enright, 2012). He also provided thought-provoking questions for each step to encourage self-assessments, a few of which I have included here. (The resources listed at the end of this chapter can help you learn more about this process.) The four steps, and self-assessment questions for each step, are as follows:

1. *Uncovering:* The victim confronts the offense directly and sees the true consequences of the injury. For example, the victim

might accept the anger of being a victim, experience changes in their view of the world, and see the connection between not forgiving and harm to oneself. Have you faced your wounds and admitted their existence? Have you been thinking, over and over, about the person and the event?

2. *Decision:* The victim, with an accurate understanding of the offense and a full acceptance of their justifiable responses, decides to forgive the offender. This decision belongs to the victim and cannot be forced by someone else. The victim sees forgiveness as the option that will lead to a better future. Have you decided that what you have been doing hasn't worked?

3. *Work:* Accepting the pain and gaining a deeper understanding of the transgression is hard work and happens only over time. For example, the victim might acknowledge and accept the pain of the transgression and come to understand the influences on the offender. Are you working toward compassion?

4. *Deepening:* In this step, the victim creates a new meaning for the offense. For example, the victim might see the betrayal they forgave as enabling them to better empathize with others in similar situations. Deepening also creates a greater capacity to forgive in the future. Are you finding meaning in what you have suffered?

Forgiveness interventions teach people about forgiveness and give them an opportunity to engage in the steps of forgiveness; many studies have examined the effects of this type of treatment. A meta-analysis of published studies concluded that treatments that focused on both emotions and intentions were more effective in improving emotional health than treatments that focused only on a behavioral decision to forgive (Baskin & Enright, 2004). Another study compared women who were abused as children (physically, emotionally, sexually) who received a 24-week forgiveness intervention with others who received only education about their health condition (Lee & Enright, 2014). The women who completed the forgiveness intervention had higher scores on measures of forgiveness and emotional and physical health than the women who completed the education-only intervention.

How does the forgiveness process work in real time? First, you must be able to accurately see the offense against you. This step is hard because you need to have self-compassion to accept your responses up to now and to hold the pain of the offender's actions against you. Then, you must decide to begin the forgiveness process, which truly is a process and happens only over time. There are several workbooks in the Resources section at the end of this chapter that can walk you through the process, but in general, you must reduce your negative feelings and motivations toward the offender and increase your positive or neutral feelings and motivations. You may have to give up your hope of an apology or even an acknowledgment of the event: This is a barrier that is quite high for many survivors. Your path to forgiveness likely won't be a smooth one, from wound to forgiveness, but rather a back-and-forth journey. One thing that might happen is that you forgive, but then at a later point in time you learn more information about the offender, or the abuse, and your forgiveness is challenged. You then need to go back and appraise the situation with this new information and move through the process again.

To summarize, here is what we know about learning to forgive:

- Forgiveness for transgressions is a process, not a one-time event. It requires a focus on the pain of the transgression as well as an increase in compassion and empathy for the offender.
- Forgiveness is a skill that can be taught and learned. People who complete training to help them forgive serious offenses experience greater forgiveness motivations and improved emotional and physical well-being.

FORGIVENESS SHOULD NOT BE A BURDEN

Forgiveness is an act of strength that creates freedom from the hold that a serious transgression has on our thoughts and feelings. However, forgiveness is also a decision you make for yourself, not one that can be made by another or imposed on you or completed within a set timeline. If you have been burdened by others' expectations for you related to forgiveness, I hope that this chapter has helped you understand forgiveness better and allowed you to fully consider it as a step in your recovery.

RESOURCES

Digital Resources

- The Forgiveness Project (https://www.theforgivenessproject. com) was founded in 2004 by journalist Marina Cantacuzino to help people who are victims or survivors and perpetrators of crime and conflict share stories of healing.

Print Resources

- *Forgive to Live Workbook*, by Dick Tibbits (Florida Hospital Publishing, 2016). This workbook is very practical and is based on a program offered to patients to help them increase forgiveness and process anger to reduce blood pressure. It outlines a 6-week program that can be used in a group setting as well as individually.
- *Forgiveness Is a Choice*, by Robert Enright (American Psychological Association, 2001). This book explains the steps of forgiveness and covers related topics, such as helping children forgive and exploring the option of reconciling.

- *Forgiveness Workbook*, by Eileen Barker (Dialogue Press, 2009). This workbook examines forgiveness and provides many exercises and activities to help readers understand and adopt a forgiveness response in a guided sequential manner. For example, one of the steps is "deconstruct your story." There is also a CD with a forgiveness meditation.
- *Let Forgiveness Set You Free*, by Meredith Hooke (Adams Media, 2021). This workbook provides a step-by-step process for forgiveness, primarily through exercises and self-assessments. It is intended for people in general, not just those who have experienced interpersonal traumas, but it is helpful in outlining many aspects of forgiveness.
- *The Forgiveness Journey Workbook*, by Nella Coiro (Sunrise Valley Publishers, 2019). Many exercises, self-assessments, guided journaling, and reflection questions are contained in this workbook. Although directed toward forgiveness in general, the "unpacking" of forgiveness will be helpful to survivors.

CHAPTER 10

HOPE

Recovery Milestones

This chapter will help you

1. **understand** the true meaning of hope,
2. **learn** how hope helps in recovery, and
3. **identify** ways you can increase hope in your life.

It is interesting what metaphors we use for concepts that are hard to explain. Sometimes a picture of something real can illustrate something that cannot be seen. So I might say I was "weighed down" by my depression, and my picture is that I have a heavy weight on my back forcing me to lean over. Or my fear was a "big, black hole" next to me that I might fall into. What is your picture of hope? Is it a feather blowing away in the breeze? Is hope a butterfly ahead of you, silhouetted against a sunset? As you read this chapter, I want you to picture in your mind a bridge, solid, strong, and beautiful. Hope is that bridge for you, and it leads from where you are standing right now to where you want to be standing next.

Along with many other concepts in this book, the scientific study of hope was invigorated when positive psychology began considering concepts associated with a meaningful life. Psychology's view is that hope is a solid concept—a plan—rather than a wish or a desire. Hope is centered in your thoughts, rather than in your feelings. A wonderful picture of hope was offered by Karl Menninger (1959): "Hope is an adventure, a going forward, a confident search" (p. 484). Psychology has much to say about hope, including its important role in recovery.

WHAT IS HOPE?

We begin with hope theory, outlined by Rick Snyder, a social psychologist. According to Snyder (2002), hope starts with goals. *Goals* are targets toward which we aim. A goal can be a thought (I would like to lose weight), a picture (me playing with a dog in the snow), or a specific objective (earn a 5% raise at work this year). Goals can be positive (I want to achieve this) and negative (I want to avoid that). Goals can be near or far, short term or long term. Goals organize our lives to bring about desired outcomes.

Pathways are trails along which we travel to reach the goal. When we think about a goal, we may define one pathway or several pathways. For example, if my goal is losing weight, my pathways could be joining a gym, using an online app to track food intake and exercise, joining an interactive program such as Weight Watchers or Noom, using a meal kit delivery service, or following a specific diet plan like the Mediterranean diet. Snyder believed it is important to identify several pathways so we have options when a pathway does not work out.

When we believe we can travel those pathways to reach the goal, we have agency. *Agency* is the conviction that we have the ability, time, resources, motivation, energy, and skills to travel the pathway and reach the goal. Because pathways can be blocked, agency is also the conviction that we can overcome the barrier or that we can pivot and find a new pathway. Returning to my weight loss goal, my agency is different for the various pathways. I have the most agency for interactive programs such as Weight Watchers and Noom because they incorporate support and structure. I have the least agency for joining a gym because of its cost and lack of accountability. The hope process unfolds as the person chooses a valued goal. (Snyder, 2002, believed that goals need to be important to the person for hope theory to apply.) When the goal is identified, the person begins to consider pathways. Part of that consideration is agency because pathways that exceed the person's capability or resources are not an option. There is a back-and-forth process, thinking about pathways and considering agency, then thinking about other pathways and agency, and so on. Eventually the person begins to travel a selected pathway toward the specific goal.

It is unlikely that the pathway will be barrier free. When the person encounters a barrier along the way, emotions are generated that feed back into agency. Most of us experience negative emotions in the face of stressors, and those negative emotions can reduce our agency. But if we start with high levels of hope, we might see those same barriers as challenges we can overcome. Alternatively, we may decide that a pathway is truly not going to be successful; then, if we are high in hope, we turn quickly to select another pathway without engaging in damaging self-criticism.

Psychologists have completed many studies of hope. Hope predicts better academic performance among college students, success in competitions for athletes, and positive adjustment in adults experiencing serious illnesses such as lung cancer and muscular dystrophy. Hope creates a range of positive emotions, including happiness and life satisfaction. Hope also is active in day-to-day life. For example, a recent study of 250 African American college students considered whether hope changed their positive and negative adjustment in the face of racial discrimination (Chang et al., 2019). When students had higher scores on hope (pathways and agency), they reported less negative adjustment (depression and anxiety) and more positive adjustment (vitality and life satisfaction) after experiences of racial discrimination. Snyder developed a measure of hope, which is in Self-Assessment 10.1.

We turn next to the experience of people struggling with chronic pain, of uncertain or unknown cause, and with low likelihood of recovery, to better understand despair. The concept of hope is central to life, but so is its opposite, despair. Despair is more likely to be your companion than hope. So it is important to learn about hope from the perspective of people who are experiencing despair. Three scientists studying two treatments for chronic pain interviewed participants over time, before starting treatment as well as during and after treatment (Eaves et al., 2016). After analyzing these interview narratives (answers), the authors identified four dimensions of hope: (a) cognitive experience, (b) experience of faith, (c) embodied experience, and (d) work.

Hope Is a Cognitive Experience

Part of the experience of hope among these chronic pain patients was cognitive, meaning that hope existed in their thoughts. One example of that cognitive experience was realistic hope. With realistic hope, these people believed in the possibility of change, while also remembering that the likelihood of change was low. Another way of thinking about realistic hope is that you hold both hope and hopelessness at the same time. A second example of the cognitive experience of hope was developing a view of a possible future and being able to envision what that future would look like.

Hope Is an Experience of Faith

Another part of the experience of hope among these chronic pain patients was faith. One example was religious or spiritual faith, such

Self-Assessment 10.1

Hope

The statements listed below describe components of hope. In your journal or note-taking app, write down the number that indicates how accurately each statement describes you using this scale: 1 = *definitely false*, 2 = *mostly false*, 3 = *mostly true*, and 4 = *definitely true*.

1. I can think of many ways to get out of a jam.
2. I energetically pursue my goals.
3. There are lots of ways around any problem.
4. I can think of many ways to get the things in life that are most important to me.
5. Even when others get discouraged, I can find a way to solve a problem.
6. My past experiences have prepared me well for the future.
7. I've been pretty successful in life.
8. I meet the goals that I set for myself.

Add up your scores in the following categories:

- Agency: Items 2, 6, 7, and 8
- Pathways: Items 1, 3, 4, and 5.

Then add the two category scores together for a total score, which will be between 8 and 32. One study found that the average total score of adults who had experienced abuse as children was 14, whereas the average score of nonabused adults was 21. How do these scores compare to yours?

Write out your reactions to these items and your scores. Was your score higher for agency—the will to achieve a goal—or pathways—the ability to identify ways to reach a goal? How do you see these concepts in your current life?

From "The Will and the Ways: Development and Validation of an Individual-Differences Measure of Hope," by C. R. Snyder, C. Harris, J. R. Anderson, S. A. Holleran, L. M. Irving, S. T. Sigmon, L. Yoshinobu, J. Gibb, C. Langelle, and P. Harney, 1991, *Journal of Personality and Social Psychology, 60*(4), p. 585 (https://doi.org/10.1037/0022-3514.60.4.570). Copyright 1991 by the American Psychological Association.

as faith in a loving deity or in the wholeness of life and spiritual healing. A second example was faith in their treatment; they continued to hope that medical science would provide a way to reduce their pain and restore their quality of life. *Faith* is confidence in something that is not based on proof; it occurs in the present. Hope is based in the future; it establishes goals we want to move forward to accomplish.

Hope Is an Embodied Experience

The patients also identified an embodied experience of hope, or the belief in their own body's ability to heal. This type of hope was internal, not dependent on a treatment or cure from outside themselves. People believed in their own minds and bodies as an important source of healing and recovery. This can be true for psychological issues as well: We can believe we have internal resources that will help us in times of difficulty.

Hope Is Work

Finally, these patients knew that hope was important for them and their recovery and that it would require work to maintain. They had experienced years of pain and many failed treatments. But hope meant knowing that treatments and other pain management techniques had to be continued and that they needed to keep from losing hope.

In summary, here is what we know about hope:

- Hope is more concrete than a wish: It consists of a specific goal with possible routes to reach the goal, along with confidence in our ability to successfully complete the routes.
- Even in the face of despair, hope can be maintained as a source of confidence in envisioning the future.

- Continuing to imagine a better future, and remaining open to the possibility that a better future is possible even as we doubt, is critical to our recovery.

WHAT ARE THE STAGES OF CHANGE TOWARD HOPE?

Psychologists have long considered what makes a person likely to change their behavior, especially when those changes are difficult to carry out. This question relates to hope because hope is the bridge between present and future, and the bridge is constructed with changes in attitudes or behaviors or both. In order to bring hope to life, we need a goal and pathways. The process of choosing a goal, defining pathways, and then following those pathways usually involves changes in our thoughts, feelings, and behaviors. For example, let's return to my goal of losing weight. To meet that goal, I need to change the types of food and the amount of food I eat, as well as to increase my daily exercise. Those changes are related but separate. In order to change the types of food I eat, I need to determine a way to categorize my food intake, and then I need to implement that categorization. Then I need to use that information to change the foods I select to eat. So one goal can have subgoals, all of which incorporate behavior changes.

Psychologist James Prochaska and his colleagues spent many years trying to understand how people decide to make changes and what enables them to maintain those changes. They developed a model that has been applied in many contexts, including quitting smoking or drinking, starting an exercise program, and following treatment recommendations. This model has five stages: precontemplation, contemplation, preparation, action, and maintenance (Prochaska & DiClemente, 1983).

Precontemplation: "I Can't Change" or "I Won't Change"

In precontemplation, the person has not yet truly considered change. If pressed, they might say that others have been suggesting change, but they don't agree that a change is needed. The person may be ignoring evidence that something is wrong so they don't have to deal with it, or they may have tried enough times to make changes that they are demoralized and do not believe that any changes will work.

Contemplation: "I Might Change"

Once the person believes there is a situation for which a change is needed, contemplation happens. The person tries to understand the situation, thinks about possible solutions, gathers information, and so on. They must also consider possible obstacles or barriers to the change and how those barriers might be overcome. This stage corresponds to Snyder's (2002) concept of identifying pathways to a goal within the context of agency.

Preparation: "I Will Change"

Once the person has decided to change, they take responsibility for the change and choose a goal and pathways. But they still have not attempted to reach that goal. In the preparation stage, they develop support for the change and, equally important, move away from social influences that might prevent it.

Action: "I Am Changing"

In the action stage, the person has started the plan. But there are slipups and problems along the way. An important part of this stage is having the confidence to approach change in new ways when initial ways are not working. Barriers can be overcome with alternative pathways to reach the goal, identified during the contemplation stage. The person also has successes in seeing their behavior change that keep them working toward the goal.

Maintenance: "I Am Still Changing"

Changing behaviors, thoughts, or feelings takes time, and the person needs to continue using change strategies for many weeks or months. That extended effort can be discouraging, and the person may struggle to keep the change going. But at this stage, the changes have been made, and the person is better off than before starting to change.

WHAT ABOUT HOPE AFTER CHILDHOOD SEXUAL ABUSE?

When you think about hope after childhood sexual abuse, it is important to keep in mind what that abuse did to your childhood development. If you did not read that material in Chapter 1, here is a summary. During normal childhood development, the child accomplishes a series of tasks, some physical, like learning to walk, and some psychological, like getting along with others and having feelings of accomplishment. Each of the stages of development between birth and young adulthood is harmed by abuse. The child does not develop autonomy (independence), feels like a failure, believes their failures are not going to change, and experiences confusion and doubt about identity. As we know from earlier in this chapter, hope is a plan based on pathways and agency. Each part, pathways and agency, is affected by damage to development. For example, the growing child feels like a failure, and that self-concept continues into adulthood, when it negatively affects agency.

A study of adults asked them to identify their experiences of childhood abuse and to complete the hope scale that is in

Self-Assessment 10.1 (Baxter et al., 2017). Adults who experienced both physical and sexual abuse as children had significantly lower hope scores than adults who had not been abused. The average score of the abused adults was 14, whereas the average score of the non-abused adults was 21. The authors noted that the combination of childhood trauma and low levels of hope as an adult meant that the abused adults had no confidence in making changes, no confidence that the environment would help maintain changes, and no commitment to making an effort to change. Thus, we know that as adults, our hope is still affected by childhood sexual abuse. The challenge therefore is to understand how we can use what we know about hope to help in our recovery.

In an extensive study of women who experienced sexual assault as a child, an adult, or both, survivors provided information on hope and their healing journeys (Saint Arnault & Sinko, 2019). Two hundred women who had experienced sexual assault completed questionnaires about the impact of their trauma, their history of childhood sexual abuse, their hope, and their posttraumatic growth. Of these women, 24 also participated in an in-person interview.

These survivors explained three ways in which hope assisted in their recovery. First, hope contributed to their relationship with themselves; the women talked about practicing self-acceptance and self-compassion. Second, hope contributed to a new identity; the women described how hope led to rebuilding their identity, learning what their strengths were, and finding their voice. The third contribution from hope was engagement; the women felt that they belonged to a community and had built trust with other people.

The authors compared the adjustment, including posttraumatic growth, of the women who had experienced both childhood sexual abuse and adult sexual assault and the women who had experienced only adult sexual assault. Although it might seem intuitive that survivors of both types of abuse had equally poor adjustment, in fact it was not so. The survivors of both childhood sexual abuse and assault as adults reported more posttraumatic growth, more self-compassion, and more resilience than the survivors of adult assault only. These survivors of childhood sexual abuse thus experienced posttraumatic growth after their repeated abuse and were able to identify new strengths.

As these research findings illustrate, hope is how we see ourselves. If we see that we have potential for change, if we believe we can identify pathways toward our goals for which we have agency, if we accurately understand our own stage of change, we have hope as a bridge to the future.

WHAT ROLE DO POSSIBLE SELVES PLAY IN HOPE?

We turn again to the concept of possible selves. Possible selves were introduced in Chapter 3 because they are relevant to our recovery journey. They are also integral to hope.

As humans, we try to make sense of our lives. We think of ourselves in terms of identities or self-concepts, or ways in which we understand ourselves in the larger surroundings of our lives. We also have *possible selves*, or ways in which we think about our future—what we would like to become, what we might become, and what we fear becoming. But over time, a possible self becomes embedded in how we see ourselves now, and thus we are becoming something all the time. That outcome happens in a variety of ways. If I want a possible self of confidence rather than fear, I might take my current experiences and hold them up to the mirror of confidence. I know what I want to be, but how is my current life helping me achieve that?

Although it makes sense that desired possible selves are influential in our lives, it is important to note that feared possible selves,

207

the selves we do not want to become, also have an influence. People who are deeply distressed by possible selves may begin to actually fear the self. We might do this when our current self demonstrates to us that we have qualities we dread having. *Fear of self* is a group of thoughts that include self-blame, shame, guilt, and a sense of personal inadequacy. If this concept sounds familiar to you, you can complete the fear of self measure in Self-Assessment 10.2.

We all have a large pool of possible selves. We look at those selves through various lenses, such as desirability and probability. *Desirability* is preference, the "I want to be" self. *Probability* is likelihood, the "I can be" self. The possible selves that are both desirable and probable are the ones toward which we aim. In the language of hope theory, those selves are our goals.

How do you move toward your best possible selves? Psychologists have tested a method for doing exactly that: taking 20 minutes each day for 2 weeks to engage in writing and actively visualizing having achieved one's best possible selves. One study that found that this method resulted in more optimism and more positive emotions (Meevissen et al., 2011). Here are the instructions, adapted from that study:

> Your best possible self means imagining yourself in a future where everything has turned out as good as possible. You have worked hard and have managed to achieve all your life goals. You can envision your best possible self as satisfying all your life dreams and developing all your best possible potentials. You have probably never thought about yourself this way. But research shows that this method may have a positive influence on your mood. (Meevissen et al., 2011, p. 377)

Think of and write down your goals for your best possible self in areas of your life such as personal, relationships, work, physical and mental health, and so on. Then merge these goals into a diary or

Self-Assessment 10.2

Fear of Self

The statements listed below reflect fear of self, which includes self-blame, shame, guilt, and a sense of personal inadequacy. In your journal or note-taking app, rate your level of agreement or disagreement with the statements using this scale: 1 = *strongly disagree*, 2 = *disagree*, 3 = *somewhat disagree*, 4 = *somewhat agree*, 5 = *agree*, 6 = *strongly agree*.

1. I often question my own character.
2. I can easily imagine myself as the kind of person who should definitely feel guilty.
3. I often question my own sanity.
4. I am sometimes afraid to look inside of myself because I am afraid of what I might find.
5. I worry about being the sort of person who might do very immoral things.
6. I am afraid of the kind of person I might become if I am not very careful.
7. I often feel that I do not honestly show the negative reality inside of me.
8. I must be very careful in order to avoid doing something awful.

In your journal or note-taking app, write down whether you think the concept of fear of self seems applicable to you. One way to do that is pick the one or two items that are most like you. Do you think that feared possible selves have an influence on whether or how you set goals?

journal that is written as if you have already achieved all these goals. What would your life be like?

In summary, here is what we know about hope after childhood sexual abuse:

- Research on adult survivors shows that they score lower on a measure of hope than do adults who were not abused in childhood.
- Research on adult survivors also shows that hope influences their positive adjustment, which includes better mood, less depression, fewer problem behaviors, and more life satisfaction.
- It is possible to have high levels of hope as a survivor; hope means having goals, pathways, and agency.

BACK TO THE BRIDGE

Let's go back to the bridge picture described at the beginning of the chapter. Hope is that strong, secure, beautiful bridge from here to someplace else in your life. Because hope is such an important part of recovery, it is worth your effort to think about your best possible selves, to select important goals and work toward reaching them, and to find yourself increasingly using hope as a resource for recovery. The resources listed next provide more readings and exercises to help you in that process.

RESOURCES

Print Resources

- *Hope Rising: How the Science of Hope Can Change Your Life*, by Casey Gwinn and Chan Hellman (Morgan James Publishing, 2019). This book applies research on hope in dealing directly with how to create more hope even after trauma. Topics covered include hope in the brain, hope after trauma, hope after shame, and a hope-centered life.

- *Making Hope Happen: Create the Future You Want for Yourself and Others*, by Shane Lopez (Atria, 2014). The author is a psychologist who has conducted extensive research on hope. He translates what he has found into user-friendly information on hope and strategies for increasing hope. This book was written not for trauma survivors, but rather for anyone who needs help increasing their hope.
- *The Confidence Gap: A Guide to Overcoming Fear and Self-Doubt*, by Russ Harris (Trumpeter Press, 2011). This book presents techniques for overcoming anxiety when starting something new. It especially focuses on thoughts that interfere with confidence. Exercises help the reader create a new understanding of and response to fear and anxiety.

CHAPTER 11

THRIVING

Recovery Milestones

This chapter will help you

1. **understand** thriving,
2. **integrate** what you learned in previous chapters, and
3. **begin** to construct your strengths portfolio.

Darin Strauss is an accomplished American author whose work has won many awards. He has written fiction, but he is also known for his 2010 memoir *Half a Life*. The title refers to the fact that his life was divided into "before" and "after," separated by an automobile accident in which he was the driver that killed a high school classmate. His account describes familiar characteristics of trauma: immobilization, intense emotional distress, isolation from present-centered living. He includes details illustrating how challenging the "after" period was, how dense the darkness, and how unlikely thriving seemed to be. Nevertheless, on his journey to finding meaning from that event, he found hope and forgave himself, learning how to thrive during darkness.

Does "thriving" sound like too much for you? Do you see yourself, instead, as languishing? Sitting on the couch, eating and drinking and using too much, feeling hopeless and demoralized, frightened of the darkness within you? It is true that some demands exceed our resources. But those overwhelming demands are far fewer than you believe. Instead, in the face of adversity, you can learn to thrive. That is the focus of this chapter. It presents information on thriving, and it takes concepts from the previous chapters and applies them to thriving. If you are reading this chapter first, or after a few of the earlier chapters, you will still find information that helps you. But the chapter will make the most sense and be most helpful if you have already understood and applied to yourself the concepts covered so far: recovery, resilience, grief, meaning, spirituality, connection, forgiveness, and hope.

WHAT IS THRIVING?

We know from research, and from our own experience, that mental health is more than the absence of mental illness, just as physical health is more than the absence of disease. Corey Keyes is a sociologist who studies human values most conducive to thriving, and he founded a center for that work (http://www.compassion.life.edu). In his analysis, he argued that thriving consists of several types of experience (Keyes, 2002). One type is emotional well-being, which is not hedonism or simple pleasure, but, rather, life satisfaction and meaning. Another type is intellectual well-being, which is self-acceptance, mastery (what he calls managing the tasks of everyday life), personal growth, and autonomy. And a third type is social well-being, which is social contribution (creating something worthwhile in one's social community) and social integration (being close to others).

How does thriving fit in the range of responses to adversity? When adversity happens, the individual is challenged on a physical level, a psychosocial level, or both. One outcome is a continual downward slope, in which the individual experiences an initial negative response to adversity that is compounded and multiplied, creating a lasting surrender. A second outcome is survival with impairment. In this situation, the individual experiences the same initial negative response, but then reverses that trend, although not to the level of their life before the challenge. There remain damages in physical or psychosocial functioning or both. A third outcome is resilience, in which the individual returns either rapidly or gradually to the level of functioning before the challenge. The fourth outcome is thriving, termed "posttraumatic growth" when the adversity is a trauma, in which the individual not only returns to the prechallenge level of functioning but surpasses it in some way.

How does that process work? Through adversity, we gather either specific skills or increased knowledge that create fuel for the growth. If we navigate a problem successfully, or even with partial success, we are more ready to deal with that problem again or with similar problems. Sometimes adversity allows or requires us to rely on others for help, advice, support, or encouragement. After the challenge, we have a better social network. And we know that from posttraumatic growth, one outcome is an increased appreciation of the strengths we identified during the adversity.

Before I give you my definition of thriving, use your journal or note-taking app to write out your own definition of thriving. Think of yourself and your own life, and write your definition of what thriving would be if you could say of yourself, "I am thriving."

Here is my definition: *Thriving* is lasting positive change after adversity, whether the adversity is unwanted or chosen, that transforms us internally (for example, increased self-acceptance, meaningful spirituality), physically (for example, new skills and abilities), and/or interpersonally (for example, more empathy, purposeful connections). Thriving creates new stories of the adversity in our past that describe characteristics of the successful journey ahead.

In summary, here is what we know about thriving:

- Thriving is a path of recovery from adversity, challenge, or trauma, with significant gains in well-being. That path contrasts with other paths after adversity that do not lead to regained function or that only return to the pretrauma normal.
- Thriving takes place in emotions, thoughts, physical health, intellectual functioning, and interpersonal connections.

IS THERE THRIVING AFTER CHILDHOOD SEXUAL ABUSE?

When I titled this chapter "Thriving," I had many moments of doubt. How is it possible to consider thriving as a possible state of being for adults who were victimized by childhood sexual abuse? Most of us are familiar with the path from victim to survivor. The term "victim" for childhood abuse survivors is meant to designate that we were truly victims, that we could not stop the abuse, and that we will not be blamed for it. "Survivor" suggests a move from being a victim to an identity that is new and fused with our recovery. Thriving takes surviving one step further: It takes our experiences and makes from them a source of vitality and renewal.

In scientific studies, we can find real-life models of people who have been able to thrive despite what happened to them as children. For example, a large team of researchers interviewed 44 women survivors of childhood sexual abuse who identified themselves as successful (J. M. Hall et al., 2009). The goal of the study was to better understand what strategies had led to success within this group of women. (Although the women defined themselves as successful, they reported a range of ongoing difficulties related to the childhood abuse, including physical health problems, depression and anxiety, flashbacks, and substance abuse.)

The narratives from the interviews allowed the researchers to outline a distinct process linked with thriving that they called "becoming resolute": "Becoming resolute was a process of developing decisive agency and a steely willfulness in refusing to be defined by or focused on one's abuse history" (J. M. Hall et al., 2009, p. 378). The steps in the process are described below. It will help you personalize these results if you use your journal or note-taking app to pause after each step is described and write out whether or how you see that step in your life. It is possible that you might identify a step as a goal.

- *Determined decisiveness:* The participants put all their energy toward taking responsibility for themselves. That did not happen easily, and many participants repeatedly tried different ways to overcome their life problems. As one participant put it, "I am learning to captain my own ship." But ultimately this step meant that the survivors accepted that their healing would be under their own control and that they could not depend on outside forces to help them achieve it.

- *Counterframing:* Counterframing was the process in which participants accepted that the negative pictures with which they viewed their childhoods—such as being frozen in the snow, being in hell, or being in prison—did not have to continue to be their adult pictures of being in the world. Counterframing was the gradual realization that they could have a new and different way of being. And they were able to change the picture of their childhood life into a new picture of an adult life.

- *Facing down death:* All the participants faced death of a sort when they saw that the abuse would lead to their own destruction. Some participants had dealt with this "existential death" using self-injurious behaviors such as substance abuse, eating disorders, and self-harm. But in the process of becoming resolute, all survivors had identified ways of healthfully coping with their struggles, including creating and experiencing art, engaging in advocacy (speaking out for others), and using meaning making as a life tool.

- *Renaming and redefining family:* Becoming resolute meant renaming their abusers as who they were—sick, violent, criminal individuals. Strengthening the boundaries between themselves and their abusers meant allowing them to move away from abusive or unsupportive family members. The survivors also identified individuals in their social network who were unsupportive or even hurtful, and moved away from those relationships as well.

- *Quest for learning:* Engaging in a continual quest for learning helped survivors find inspiration. Many participants reported being book lovers, finding their inspiration in female heroines and books with justice themes. Other sources were films and shows, self-help books, and education. Many of the participants returned to school at nontraditional ages or took courses that gave them new skills or a new appreciation for subjects such as history or literature or the arts.

- *Moving beyond:* Participants reported that thriving meant literally moving past a line they drew between their abuse and their current lives. Because the abuse began so early (36% of the participants reported abuse before age 7), the lack of a normal childhood prevented their having a "normal" to which they could return. Therefore, they saw their moving beyond the line of their past as an act of self-construction, one over which they had control and ability.

Let's look back and apply several concepts or strategies we identified in previous chapters to thriving. We have explored possible selves in several chapters. One way to move toward thriving is to use your *best possible selves*. Briefly, they are our ideal selves when we have satisfied all our life dreams and developed all our potentials.

A treatment to help you define and use best possible selves has you write in your journal or note-taking app for 20 minutes each day for 2 weeks. The key is to write each entry as if you had already accomplished your best possible selves (for a deeper description, see Chapter 10). A recent study (Heekerens & Heinitz, 2019) examined the effect of the writing "as if" treatment on thriving. Participants who completed the best possible selves intervention scored higher on thriving after that treatment; participants also reported liking the treatment and finding it beneficial. The ways in which the participants interacted with their best possible selves diaries were by writing them, rereading them to themselves and out loud, visualizing them, and elaborating on them.

Another concept with a relationship to thriving is *self-compassion*. We have examined self-compassion in previous chapters. Briefly, self-compassion is both the ability and the decision to be kind to oneself in times of difficulty (such as failure) or despair. Self-compassion includes self-kindness, which is being supportive and positive toward oneself rather than harshly self-critical. It includes connection and the recognition that all of humanity is imperfect and that our errors are of a kind with everyone else. It also includes mindfulness, which helps us be able and willing to tolerate negative emotions without binding to them.

Although self-compassion might sound like something you either "have" or "don't have," you can acquire and increase self-compassion. Many counselors have been using treatments to help people increase their self-compassion. These treatments have several commonalities. First, they educate participants about self-compassion, including how early life experiences shaped their tendencies away from self-compassion toward harsh self-criticism. Second, they build skills related to self-compassion, such as managing difficult emotions and applying self-compassion to various challenges. Third, they result in an identity that is self-compassionate, moving away from self-blame and guilt toward the core value of acceptance.

Do these treatments work? Several researchers conducted a meta-analysis of published studies on these treatments to determine outcomes that occurred across individual studies (Ferrari et al., 2019). They analyzed results from 27 studies with a total of 1,480 participants. The most important finding was that self-compassion increased after several types of treatment, for participants of many different ages, who came to treatment with a variety of mental health and behavioral issues. Treatments for self-compassion were also found to have additional benefits; for example, stress, depression, and anxiety were reduced.

A third concept with a relationship to thriving is *emotional regulation*. Emotional regulation is the process of using your emotions in the service of achieving a desired state. Most, if not all, survivors have difficulty with our emotions. We cannot identify them, we are overwhelmed by them, and we are frightened of them. Most survivors have developed ways of dealing with emotions that create additional problems: They avoid them or numb them using strategies such as restrictive eating and other eating patterns that develop into eating disorders, self-harm, abuse of alcohol and other drugs, compulsive behaviors such as shopping and gambling, and deadening emotions altogether.

Psychologists have written about emotional regulation, and their views help us better understand it. Aaron and colleagues (2020) saw emotional regulation as having three stages: emotional identification, strategy selection, and strategy implementation. In everyday terms, that is knowing how you feel, deciding what to do about it, and doing that. Emotional regulation strategies generally either decrease (minimize or shrink) emotions or increase (activate or enhance) emotions. In Chapter 4, we explored the broaden and build model, in which positive emotions stimulate increased flexibility and creativity in responses, which then further increase positive emotions. The visual model of this process is an upward spiral.

How do you know how you feel? Unfortunately, knowing how we feel is quite difficult for survivors. Because in our past it was not safe to know how we felt, we deliberately avoided knowing. That strategy led to *alexithymia*, which is the inability to know how we feel. The tasks we face in this stage are being aware of our emotions, giving them the correct label, and differentiating one emotion from another. The resources listed at the end of this chapter can help you with these tasks.

Accurate identification of emotions leads to effective regulation strategies. One example of a strategy is cognitive reappraisal. This strategy involves identifying thoughts that work against us (for example, catastrophizing or suppressing) and replacing them with more adaptive thoughts (including effective problem solving and confidence building). Another strategy is based in mindfulness and involves engaging with our difficult emotions in a different way. Examples are slowing ourselves down with breathing and allowing our emotions to occur without being fused with them.

In summary, here is what we know about thriving among adults who experienced childhood sexual abuse:

- Research tells us that adults can thrive even though they experience difficulties characteristic of adult survivors of childhood sexual abuse. They achieved this outcome through a series of processes, or pathways, that led them to make decisions related to their recovery needs and implement them.
- An example of a step toward thriving is the decision to rename and redefine your "family" so that you can find and maintain healthy relationships and identify and terminate abusive relationships.
- Three examples of concepts we discussed earlier in this book that relate to thriving are best possible selves, or seeing the potential of having met life goals and achieved life dreams;

221

self-compassion, or being kind to oneself; and emotional regulation, or knowing and accepting and managing both positive and negative emotions.

PORTFOLIO BUILDING

What is a portfolio? In everyday language, a portfolio is a collection. An artist would have a portfolio of finished works. A musician would have a portfolio of compositions. An architect would have a portfolio of building designs. And you are about to have a portfolio of strengths.

Psychologists who study trauma, including violence, developed the "resilience portfolio model," and that is the model we will use for developing your portfolio of strengths (Hamby et al., 2018, 2020). Their model is based on the idea that we have a portfolio of strengths, some stronger and others less so, with more strengths or fewer strengths overall. There are two general types of portfolio. The first is a portfolio with different strengths, termed "poly-strengths." These strengths are at a moderate to high level. The second is a portfolio with fewer strengths that operate at a high level, termed "signature strengths"; these are the two to four strengths most characteristic of you, the ones you turn to in challenging situations. Your portfolio is likely to consist of either poly-strengths or signature strengths.

Take a minute now and look back at the self-assessment of strengths you completed in Chapter 3 (Self-Assessment 3.2). To remind you, strengths cluster in distinct categories. (And recall that we have not covered all the strengths measured by that self-assessment in this book.) Those categories are wisdom and knowledge (example strengths are love of learning and creativity), courage (example strengths are persistence and bravery), humanity (example strengths are kindness and love), justice (example strengths are fairness and leadership), temperance (example strengths are forgiveness and humility), and transcendence (example strengths are hope and spirituality). If you did not complete that self-assessment, please do it now because you will want that information for this chapter. If you did complete the self-assessment, look over your results again and consider whether your portfolio consists of poly-strengths or signature strengths.

The second part of the resilience portfolio model is that the strengths you have will help you after trauma along three pathways to thriving. One pathway is emotional regulation. This pathway helps you deal directly with the trauma itself—for example, managing distressing emotions or using persistence to maintain your coping. A second pathway is meaning making. This pathway helps you deal with the trauma by changing your perspective on it. You may change from being trapped inside by your trauma to seeing ways you have become a better person. A third pathway is interpersonal connection. This pathway helps you deal with the trauma through social support, either by obtaining it for yourself or by providing care and guidance to other people.

This is a complicated model, so let me put it in different terms. This model of thriving says that everyone has a portfolio or collection of strengths. You might have a poly-strengths portfolio, meaning that you have more strengths at a moderate level. Or you might have a signature strengths portfolio, meaning that you have fewer strengths but at a high level. No matter how many strengths you have, and how strong they are, your strengths help you in a variety of ways. Some strengths help you regulate: That is, they help you manage distressing emotions, thoughts, and behaviors by allowing them to exist without being overwhelmed by them. Some strengths transform you: Ways of being transformed include spirituality, meaning making, and grief. Other strengths help you approach others and make connections, allowing others to learn from you.

What is important is that strengths operate on one or more of the pathways to thriving. Let me use my own experience to show you how that works. One of my strengths is spirituality, a signature strength. This strength contributes to meaning making by giving me a larger context for my experience of abuse and to regulation by helping me deal with emotions related to abuse. Another signature strength is courage. I stand up for what I think is right, even if that is not an option that others appreciate. As you might expect, honesty is a third signature strength. If I put courage and honesty at the top of my portfolio, what effect do they have on my recovery journey? For emotional regulation, those strengths can hurt. I feel it deeply when I believe I or others are treated unfairly. That means I get angry and have difficulty regulating it. So I need to set a goal for myself of using that strength in a mindful way, allowing those emotions to exist but not being bound up in them.

The developers of the resilience portfolio model have investigated it with adults and adolescents after trauma (all types, not just sexual abuse; Hamby et al., 2018, 2020). Of relevance to this chapter, they studied which strengths were most useful in creating conditions that led to thriving. The most important strengths were endurance (bravery and persistence), emotional awareness, purpose (wisdom), generativity (love and kindness), and compassion; these terms are from the VIA Character Strengths Survey, a tool you can use to assess your strengths (see the Resources section at the end of this chapter). The single strength that was most helpful was sense of purpose.

An important question as you set up your portfolio is whether it is better to rely on your signature strengths for every challenge or to try to develop some strengths you don't currently have. A study relevant to this question compared these two approaches in two treatments for personal growth (Meyers et al., 2015). One treatment helped participants identify strengths that they were not comfortable using or did not think they had. Once those deficiencies were identified, the participants used goal setting to pick strengths to increase and then participated in activities to increase those strengths. The other treatment helped participants identify their most prominent strengths and then learn to use them in new ways. The treatment that resulted in more personal growth overall and an increase in hope was the treatment that taught participants to use their prominent strengths in different ways. That result suggests that instead of trying to develop personal strengths you wish you had, you should learn to use the strengths you already have more effectively. The website that contains the VIA Character Strengths Survey has many resources that can help you do this.

Let us recall why the resilience portfolio approach to healing from childhood sexual abuse is important. Up until about 10 years ago, the dominant treatments were focused on identifying the problematic symptoms of posttraumatic stress disorder, reducing those symptoms, and returning survivors to their previous level of functioning. This model viewed survivors as "problem-ridden, powerless, and in need of repair" (Walker-Williams & Fouché, 2018, p. 1). Since then, treatments have increasingly used a strengths-based approach, which asks, "What strengths does the survivor have now, and what strengths can they develop?" This approach acknowledges that strengths can be born from struggle, and that posttraumatic growth can be an outcome of trauma.

Focusing on your portfolio of strengths involves two important steps. The first is to identify your strengths. Using a self-assessment tool is helpful, as is reading about personal strengths. Many of the materials listed in the Resources section at the end of this chapter can help with this step. The second step is to learn to apply the strengths you currently have to resolve many or most symptoms and problems stemming from your trauma. It is not so much that one or two strengths are essential; rather, many different strengths can help you.

Building your portfolio will take time. Reflecting on your strengths is difficult, especially if you do not know yourself well. It can feel strange to think about strengths when you feel defeated most of the time. You also may have been told many times that you are lacking. You may want to visualize your portfolio of strengths or your pathways to thriving in an artistic format, or you may find it helpful to develop practices that give you time and space to reflect on them. No matter what your portfolio looks like or consists of, it is yours alone.

In summary, here is what we know about building a portfolio of strengths:

- Your portfolio is your personal collection of strengths; they are components of being human that contribute to your well-being in life.
- Your portfolio may have several to many strengths—a poly-strengths portfolio. Or your portfolio may have a few very influential strengths—a signature strengths portfolio.
- The strengths in your portfolio work along one or more of three pathways to thriving: emotional regulation, meaning making, and interpersonal connection. These pathways assist your recovery from trauma.
- Your portfolio is not fixed, and you are in the process of development. For example, 5 years from now, you may have new strengths that are the result of your work on recovery.

FROM FORGIVENESS TO THRIVING

I want to close by telling you about my own experience with the strength of forgiveness. You will remember from Chapter 9 my interaction with my pastor when I told him of my childhood. But it was not just my father I needed to forgive. I also needed to forgive those in my family and among my friends who were hurtful, hateful, or both in the face of my struggles. That seemed an impossible goal that simply got more impossible as time went by and I experienced more wounding. But somewhere in there, as I got to know the information I have given you in this book, I accepted two very important truths. One was that I had enough of the strength required for forgiveness. Two was that there was no time limit for me to use it.

I used forgiveness to achieve emotional regulation, meaning making, and connection, but it was a years-long process. When I forgave others, I traveled the pathway of emotional regulation. I left bitterness and rage behind me and embraced a positive stance, or at least a neutral stance. When I forgave others, I traveled the path of meaning making. Seeing myself as a forgiving person even in the middle of the darkness that was my life gave me a new identity. I also joined new communities of faith when I forgave people from old communities of faith of which I had been a member. That was the start of my thriving. Last, when I forgave others, I traveled the path of interpersonal connection. I began advocating for others, both in my immediate life circle and in the broader world of authorship. Writing this book, for me, is on my pathway to recovery. My hope is that it helps as you walk on your own pathway.

RESOURCES

Digital Resources

- The VIA Institute on Character (http://www.viacharacter.org) is the website for the VIA Character Strengths Survey. In addition to the survey, there are many reports on character strengths, resources to educate you, and additional information on this use of positive psychology.
- Action for Happiness (https://www.actionforhappiness.org) provides a short curriculum on using character strengths with

examples of movies that illustrate each strength (https://
www.actionforhappiness.org/media/52486/340_ways_to_use_
character_strengths.pdf).

Print Resources

- *201 Positive Psychology Applications*, by Fredrike Bannink
  (Norton, 2017). This practical book discusses all of the strengths
  covered in assessments of strengths and applies them to five
  pillars of well-being—positive emotion, engagement, relationships, meaning, and accomplishment.
- *Healing From the Trauma of Childhood Sexual Abuse*, by
  Karen Duncan (Praeger Press, 2008). This book offers comprehensive content in several areas of healing. In particular,
  it deals with decisions about disclosure and covers moral, legal,
  and family issues created by disclosure.
- *Life After Trauma: A Workbook for Healing*, by Dena
  Rosenbloom and Mary Beth Williams (Guilford Press, 2010).
  This workbook begins with basic information and exercises
  about trauma. It then presents five needs—safety, trust, control, self-esteem, and intimacy—and provides opportunities to
  think through how you meet those needs.
- *Mind–Body Workbook for PTSD*, by Stanley Block and
  Carolyn Block (New Harbinger, 2010). This workbook contains a 10-week program for healing from trauma (all types
  of trauma, not necessarily childhood sexual abuse) and has
  one exercise for each day. The topics are highly relevant for
  the readers of this book, including trauma memories and negative views of the self.
- *The Happiness Trap: How to Stop Struggling and Start Living*,
  by Russ Harris (Trumpeter Books, 2008). Acceptance and commitment therapy (ACT) is an approach to stress and anxiety

that teaches you to change your relationship with your thoughts and feelings. It also focuses on identifying your values and reorienting your life around them. This book is a user-friendly guide to adding tenets of ACT to your recovery.

- *The Mind–Body Stress Reset: Somatic Practices to Reduce Overwhelm and Increase Well-Being*, by Rebekkah LaDyne (New Harbinger, 2020). "Somatic intelligence" is a term for using what is going on in your body to inform your response to difficult situations in your life. This book contains information and self-assessments for understanding how to reduce your feelings of stress.

REFERENCES

Aardema, F., Moulding, R., Radomsky, A. S., Doron, G., Allamby, J., & Souki, E. (2013). Fear of self and obsessionality: Development and validation of the Fear of Self Questionnaire. *Journal of Obsessive–Compulsive and Related Disorders*, 2(3), 306–315. https://doi.org/10.1016/j.jocrd.2013.05.005

Aaron, R. V., Finan, P. H., Wegener, S. T., Keefe, F. J., & Lumley, M. A. (2020). Emotion regulation as a transdiagnostic factor underlying co-occurring chronic pain and problematic opioid use. *American Psychologist*, 75(6), 796–810. https://doi.org/10.1037/amp0000678

American Psychiatric Association. (2013). *Diagnostic and statistical manual of mental disorders* (5th ed.). https://doi.org/10.1176/appi.books.9780890425596

Bartrés-Faz, D., Cattaneo, G., Solana, J., Tormos, J. M., & Pascual-Leone, A. (2018). Meaning in life: Resilience beyond reserve. *Alzheimer's Research & Therapy*, 10(1), 47. https://doi.org/10.1186/s13195-018-0381-z

Baskin, T. W., & Enright, R. D. (2004). Intervention studies on forgiveness: A meta-analysis. *Journal of Counseling and Development*, 82(1), 79–90. https://doi.org/10.1002/j.1556-6678.2004.tb00288.x

Bass, E., & Davis, L. (2008). *The courage to heal*. Harper.

Baxter, M. A., Hemming, E. J., McIntosh, H. C., & Hellman, C. M. (2017). Exploring the relationship between adverse childhood experiences and hope. *Journal of Child Sexual Abuse*, 26(8), 948–956. https://doi.org/10.1080/10538712.2017.1365319

Bolen, R. M., & Lamb, J. L. (2004). Ambivalence of nonoffending guardians after child sexual abuse disclosure. *Journal of Interpersonal Violence, 19*(2), 185–211. https://doi.org/10.1177/0886260503260324

Bourdon, L. S., & Cook, A. S. (1994). Losses associated with sexual abuse: Therapist and client perceptions. *Journal of Child Sexual Abuse, 2*(4), 69–82. https://doi.org/10.1300/J070v02n04_05

Byrne, R. M. (2016). Counterfactual thought. *Annual Review of Psychology, 67,* 135–157. https://doi.org/10.1146/annurev-psych-122414-033249

Cacciatore, J. (2012). Selah: A mindfulness guide through grief. In R. A. Neimeyer (Ed.), *Techniques of grief therapy: Creative practices for counseling the bereaved* (pp. 16–19). Routledge.

Centers for Disease Control and Prevention. (2020). *Adverse childhood experiences (ACEs).* https://www.cdc.gov/violenceprevention/aces/index.html

Chang, E. C., Chang, O. D., Rollock, D., Lui, P. P., Watkins, A. F., Hirsch, J. K., & Jeglic, E. L. (2019). Hope above racial discrimination and social support in accounting for positive and negative psychological adjustment in African American adults: Is "knowing you can do it" as important as "knowing how you can"? *Cognitive Therapy and Research, 43*(2), 399–411. https://doi.org/10.1007/s10608-018-9949-y

Clark, J. L., Algoe, S. B., & Green, M. C. (2018). Social network sites and well-being: The role of social connection. *Current Directions in Psychological Science, 27*(1), 32–37. https://doi.org/10.1177/0963721417730833

Courtois, C. A. (2014). *It's not you, it's what happened to you: Complex trauma and treatment.* Elements Behavioral Health.

Cutrona, C. E., & Russell, D. (1987). The provisions of social relationships and adaptation to stress. In W. H. Jones & D. Perlman (Eds.), *Advances in personal relationships* (Vol. 1, pp. 37–67). JAI Press.

Dezutter, J., Soenens, B., & Hutsebaut, K. (2006). Religiosity and mental health: A further exploration of the relative importance of religious behaviors versus religious attitudes. *Personality and Individual Differences, 40*(4), 807–818. https://doi.org/10.1016/j.paid.2005.08.014

Douglas, E. M., & Finkelhor, D. (2005). *Childhood sexual abuse fact sheet.* Crimes Against Children Research Center. http://unh.edu/ccrc/factsheet/pdf/childhoodSexualAbuseFactSheet.pdf

Dube, S. R., Anda, R. F., Whitfield, C. L., Brown, D. W., Felitti, V. J., Dong, M., & Giles, W. H. (2005). Long-term consequences of childhood sexual abuse by gender of victim. *American Journal of Preventive Medicine*, *28*(5), 430–438. https://doi.org/10.1016/j.amepre.2005.01.015

Eaves, E. R., Nichter, M., & Ritenbaugh, C. (2016). Ways of hoping: Navigating the paradox of hope and despair in chronic pain. *Culture, Medicine and Psychiatry*, *40*(1), 35–58. https://doi.org/10.1007/s11013-015-9465-4

Enright, R. D. (2012). *The forgiving life: A pathway to overcoming resentment and creating a legacy of love*. American Psychological Association. https://doi.org/10.2307/j.ctv1chs8pg

Erikson, E. (1968). *Identity: Youth and crisis*. Norton.

Exline, J. J., Pargament, K. I., Grubbs, J. B., & Yali, A. M. (2014). The Religious and Spiritual Struggles Scale: Development and initial validation. *Psychology of Religion and Spirituality*, *6*(3), 208–222. https://doi.org/10.1037/a0036465

Fehr, R., Gelfand, M. J., & Nag, M. (2010). The road to forgiveness: A meta-analytic synthesis of its situational and dispositional correlates. *Psychological Bulletin*, *136*(5), 894–914. https://doi.org/10.1037/a0019993

Felitti, V. J., Anda, R. F., Nordenberg, D., Williamson, D. F., Spitz, A. M., Edwards, V., Koss, M. P., & Marks, J. S. (1998). Relationship of childhood abuse and household dysfunction to many of the leading causes of death in adults: The Adverse Childhood Experiences (ACE) Study. *American Journal of Preventive Medicine*, *14*(4), 245–258. https://doi.org/10.1016/S0749-3797(98)00017-8

Ferrari, M., Hunt, C., Harrysunker, A., Abbott, M. J., Beath, A. P., & Einstein, D. A. (2019). Self-compassion interventions and psychosocial outcomes: A meta-analysis of RCTs. *Mindfulness*, *10*(8), 1455–1473. https://doi.org/10.1007/s12671-019-01134-6

Finkelhor, D. (1984). *Child sexual abuse: New theory and research*. Free Press.

Fiore, J. (2019). A systematic review of the dual process model of coping with bereavement (1999–2016). *Omega*. Advance online publication. https://doi.org/10.1177/0030222819893139

Fleming, S. J., & Belanger, S. K. (2001). Trauma, grief, and surviving childhood sexual abuse. In R. A. Neimeyer (Ed.), *Meaning reconstruction and the experience of loss* (pp. 311–323). American Psychological Association. https://doi.org/10.1037/10397-016

Ford, J. (2017). Complex trauma and complex PTSD. In J. Cook, S. Gold, & C. Dalenberg (Eds.), *Handbook of trauma psychology* (Vol. 1, pp. 322–349). American Psychological Association. https://doi.org/10.1037/0000019-015

Fourie, M. M., Hortensius, R., & Decety, J. (2020). Parsing the components of forgiveness: Psychological and neural mechanisms. *Neuroscience and Biobehavioral Reviews, 112*, 437–451. https://doi.org/10.1016/j.neubiorev.2020.02.020

Frankl, V. E. (1992). *Man's search for meaning: An introduction to logotherapy* (I. Lasch, Trans., 4th ed.). Beacon Press. (Original work published 1946)

Frattaroli, J. (2006). Experimental disclosure and its moderators: A meta-analysis. *Psychological Bulletin, 132*(6), 823–865. https://doi.org/10.1037/0033-2909.132.6.823

Fredrickson, B. L. (2001). The role of positive emotions in positive psychology: The broaden-and-build theory of positive emotions. *American Psychologist, 56*(3), 218–226. https://doi.org/10.1037/0003-066X.56.3.218

Freyd, J., & Birrell, P. (2013). *Blind to betrayal: Why we fool ourselves we aren't being fooled.* John Wiley.

George, L. S., & Park, C. L. (2016). Meaning in life as comprehension, purpose, and mattering: Toward integration and new research questions. *Review of General Psychology, 20*(3), 205–220. https://doi.org/10.1037/gpr0000077

Griffin, B. J., Worthington, E. L., Jr., Lavelock, C. R., Wade, N. G., & Hoyt, W. T. (2015). Forgiveness and mental health. In L. Toussaint, E. Worthington, & D. Williams (Eds.), *Forgiveness and health: Scientific evidence and theories relating forgiveness to better health* (pp. 77–90). Springer. https://doi.org/10.1007/978-94-017-9993-5_6

Grossman, F. K., Sorsoli, L., & Kia-Keating, M. (2006). A gale force wind: Meaning making by male survivors of childhood sexual abuse. *The American Journal of Orthopsychiatry, 76*(4), 434–443. https://doi.org/10.1037/0002-9432.76.4.434

Gucciardi, D. F., Lines, R. L. J., Peeling, P., Chapman, M. T., & Temby, P. (2021). Mental toughness as a psychological determinant of behavioral perseverance in Special Forces selection. *Sport, Exercise, and Performance Psychology, 10*(1), 164–175. https://doi.org/10.1037/spy0000208

Ha, N., Bae, S. M., & Hyun, M. H. (2019). The effect of forgiveness writing therapy on posttraumatic growth in survivors of sexual abuse. *Sexual and Relationship Therapy*, *34*(1), 10–22. https://doi.org/10.1080/14681994.2017.1327712

Hall, J. M., Roman, M. W., Thomas, S. P., Travis, C. B., Powell, J., Tennison, C. R., Moyers, K., Shoffner, D. H., Bolton, K. M., Broyles, T., Martin, T., & McArthur, P. M. (2009). Thriving as becoming resolute in narratives of women surviving childhood maltreatment. *The American Journal of Orthopsychiatry*, *79*(3), 375–386. https://doi.org/10.1037/a0016531

Hall, T. A. (1995). Spiritual effects of childhood sexual abuse in adult Christian women. *Journal of Psychology and Theology*, *23*(2), 129–134. https://doi.org/10.1177/009164719502300205

Hamby, S., Grych, J., & Banyard, V. (2018). Resilience portfolios and poly-strengths: Identifying protective factors associated with thriving after adversity. *Psychology of Violence*, *8*(2), 172–183. https://doi.org/10.1037/vio0000135

Hamby, S., Taylor, E., Mitchell, K., Jones, L., & Newlin, C. (2020). Poly-victimization, trauma, and resilience: Exploring strengths that promote thriving after adversity. *Journal of Trauma & Dissociation*, *21*(3), 376–395. https://doi.org/10.1080/15299732.2020.1719261

Harris, K. A., Howell, D. S., & Spurgeon, D. W. (2018). Faith concepts in psychology: Three 30-year definitional content analyses. *Psychology of Religion and Spirituality*, *10*(1), 1–29. https://doi.org/10.1037/rel0000134

Heekerens, J. B., & Heinitz, K. (2019). Looking forward: The effect of the best-possible-self intervention on thriving through relative intrinsic goal pursuits. *Journal of Happiness Studies*, *20*(5), 1379–1395. https://doi.org/10.1007/s10902-018-9999-6

Herman, J. (1997). *Trauma and recovery: The aftermath of violence—From domestic abuse to political terror*. Basic Books.

Holmes, T. H., & Rahe, R. H. (1967). The Social Readjustment Rating Scale. *Journal of Psychosomatic Research*, *11*(2), 213–218. https://doi.org/10.1016/0022-3999(67)90010-4

Hooker, S. A., Masters, K. S., & Park, C. L. (2018). A meaningful life is a healthy life: A conceptual model linking meaning and meaning salience to health. *Review of General Psychology*, *22*(1), 11–24. https://doi.org/10.1037/gpr0000115

Houg, B. L. (2008). *The role of spirituality in the ongoing recovery process of female sexual abuse survivors* (Publication No. 3330510) [Doctoral dissertation, University of Minnesota]. ProQuest Dissertations and Theses Global.

James, W. (1902). *Varieties of religious experience: A study in human nature.* Longmans, Green and Co. https://doi.org/10.1037/10004-000

Janoff-Bulman, R. (1989). Assumptive worlds and the stress of traumatic events: Applications of the schema construct. *Social Cognition, 7*(2), 113–136. https://doi.org/10.1521/soco.1989.7.2.113

Janoff-Bulman, R. (2004). Posttraumatic growth: Three explanatory models. *Psychological Inquiry, 15*(1), 30–34. https://www.jstor.org/stable/20447198

Jeste, D. V., Savla, G. N., Thompson, W. K., Vahia, I. V., Glorioso, D. K., Martin, A. S., Palmer, B. W., Rock, D., Golshan, S., Kraemer, H. C., & Depp, C. A. (2013). Association between older age and more successful aging: Critical role of resilience and depression. *The American Journal of Psychiatry, 170*(2), 188–196. https://doi.org/10.1176/appi.ajp.2012.12030386

Keyes, C. L. M. (2002). The mental health continuum: From languishing to flourishing in life. *Journal of Health and Social Research, 43*(2), 207–222. https://doi.org/10.2307/3090197

Kia-Keating, M., Grossman, F. K., Sorsoli, L., & Epstein, M. (2005). Containing and resisting masculinity: Narratives of renegotiation among resilient male survivors of childhood sexual abuse. *Psychology of Men & Masculinity, 6*(3), 169–185. https://doi.org/10.1037/1524-9220.6.3.169

Kosarkova, A., Malinakova, K., Koncalova, Z., Tavel, P., & van Dijk, J. P. (2020). Childhood trauma is associated with the spirituality of non-religious respondents. *International Journal of Environmental Research and Public Health, 17*(4), 1268. https://doi.org/10.3390/ijerph17041268

Kosminsky, P. S. (2012). Mapping the terrain of loss: Grief and not grief. In R. A. Neimeyer (Ed.), *Techniques of grief therapy: Creative practices for counseling the bereaved* (pp. 30–32). Routledge.

Kübler-Ross, E. (1969). *On death and dying.* Routledge.

Lassri, D., Luyten, P., Fonagy, P., & Shahar, G. (2018). Undetected scars? Self-criticism, attachment, and romantic relationships among otherwise well-functioning childhood sexual abuse survivors. *Psychological*

Trauma: Theory, Research, Practice, and Policy, 10(1), 121–129. https://doi.org/10.1037/tra0000271

Leamy, M., Bird, V., LeBoutillier, C., Williams, J., & Slade, M. (2011). Conceptual framework for personal recovery in mental health: Systematic review and narrative synthesis. *The British Journal of Psychiatry, 199*(6), 445–452. https://doi.org/10.1192/bjp.bp.110.083733

Lee, Y.-R., & Enright, R. D. (2014). A forgiveness intervention for women with fibromyalgia who were abused in childhood: A pilot study. *Spirituality in Clinical Practice, 1*(3), 203–217. https://doi.org/10.1037/scp0000025

Lee, Y.-R., & Enright, R. D. (2019). A meta-analysis of the association between forgiveness of others and physical health. *Psychology & Health, 34*(5), 626–643. https://doi.org/10.1080/08870446.2018.1554185

Li, P. F. J., Wong, Y. J., & Chao, R. C. L. (2019). Happiness and meaning in life: Unique, differential, and indirect associations with mental health. *Counselling Psychology Quarterly, 32*(3–4), 396–414. https://doi.org/10.1080/09515070.2019.1604493

Lichtenthal, W. G., & Neimeyer, R. A. (2012). Directed journaling to facilitate meaning-making. In R. A. Neimeyer (Ed.), *Techniques of grief therapy* (pp. 165–168). American Psychological Association.

Lindemann, E. (1944). Symptomatology and management of acute grief. *The American Journal of Psychiatry, 101*(2), 141–148. https://doi.org/10.1176/ajp.101.2.141

Luthar, S. S., Cicchetti, D., & Becker, B. (2000). The construct of resilience: A critical evaluation and guidelines for future work. *Child Development, 71*(3), 543–562. https://doi.org/10.1111/1467-8624.00164

Maltby, J., Day, L., & Barber, L. (2004). Forgiveness and mental health variables: Interpreting the relationship using an adaptational–continuum model of personality and coping. *Personality and Individual Differences, 37*(8), 1629–1641. https://doi.org/10.1016/j.paid.2004.02.017

Markus, H., & Nurius, P. (1986). Possible selves. *The American Psychologist, 41*(9), 954–969. https://doi.org/10.1037/0003-066X.41.9.954

Markus, H., & Wurf, E. (1987). The dynamic self-concept: A social psychological perspective. *Annual Review of Psychology, 38*, 299–337. https://doi.org/10.1146/annurev.ps.38.020187.001503

Marriott, C., Hamilton-Giachritsis, C., & Harrop, C. (2014). Factors promoting resilience following childhood sexual abuse: A structured, narrative review of the literature. *Child Abuse Review, 23*(1), 17–34. https://doi.org/10.1002/car.2258

Masten, A. S., Cutuli, J. J., Herbers, J. E., & Reed, M. J. (2009). Resilience in development. In S. J. Lopez & C. R. Snyder (Eds.), *The Oxford handbook of positive psychology* (2nd ed., pp. 117–132). Oxford University Press.

Mazza, C., Ricci, E., Biondi, S., Colasanti, M., Ferracuti, S., Napoli, C., & Roma, P. (2020). A nationwide survey of psychological distress among Italian people during the COVID-19 pandemic: Immediate psychological responses and associated factors. *International Journal of Environmental Research and Public Health, 17*(9), 3165. https://doi.org/10.3390/ijerph17093165

McCubbin, L. D. (2016). *Resilience, adaptation, and well-being: The Kauai Longitudinal Study.* https://www.mccubbinresilience.org/kauai-longitudinal-study.html

McCullough, M. E., & Hoyt, W. T. (2002). Transgression-related motivational dispositions: Personality substrates of forgiveness and their links to the Big Five. *Personality and Social Psychology Bulletin, 28*(11), 1556–1573. https://doi.org/10.1177/014616702237583

McCullough, M. E., Rachal, K. C., Sandage, S. J., Worthington, E. L., Jr., Brown, S. W., & Hight, T. L. (1998). Interpersonal forgiving in close relationships: II. Theoretical elaboration and measurement. *Journal of Personality and Social Psychology, 75*(6), 1586–1603. https://doi.org/10.1037/0022-3514.75.6.1586

McGee, J. S., Zhao, H. C., Myers, D. R., & Kim, S. M. (2017). Positive psychological assessment and early-stage dementia. *Clinical Gerontologist, 40*(4), 307–319. https://doi.org/10.1080/07317115.2017.1305032

McMillen, C., Zuravin, S., & Rideout, G. (1995). Perceived benefit from child sexual abuse. *Journal of Consulting and Clinical Psychology, 63*(6), 1037–1043. https://doi.org/10.1037/0022-006X.63.6.1037

Meevissen, Y. M. C., Peters, M. L., & Alberts, H. J. E. M. (2011). Become more optimistic by imagining a best possible self: Effects of a two week intervention. *Journal of Behavior Therapy and Experimental Psychiatry, 42*(3), 371–378. https://doi.org/10.1016/j.jbtep.2011.02.012

Menninger, K. (1959). The academic lecture: Hope. *The American Journal of Psychiatry, 116*(6), 481–491. https://doi.org/10.1176/ajp.116.6.481

Meyers, M. C., van Woerkom, M., de Reuver, R. S. M., Bakk, Z., & Oberski, D. L. (2015). Enhancing psychological capital and personal growth initiative: Working on strengths or deficiencies. *Journal of Counseling Psychology, 62*(1), 50–62. https://doi.org/10.1037/cou0000050

Molzahn, A. E., Bruce, A., & Sheilds, L. (2008). Learning from stories of people with chronic kidney disease. *Nephrology Nursing Journal, 35*(1), 13–20.

Morton, K. R., Tanzini, L., & Lee, J. W. (2019). Adult life satisfaction and the role of forgiveness after childhood sexual abuse: Evidence from a Seventh Day Adventist cohort. *Journal for the Scientific Study of Religion, 58*(1), 138–152. https://doi.org/10.1111/jssr.12575

Murthi, M., & Espelage, D. L. (2005). Childhood sexual abuse, social support, and psychological outcomes: A loss framework. *Child Abuse & Neglect, 29*(11), 1215–1231. https://doi.org/10.1016/j.chiabu. 2005.03.008

Nadal, A. R. C., Hardy, S. A., & Barry, C. M. (2018). Understanding the roles of religiosity and spirituality in emerging adults in the United States. *Psychology of Religion and Spirituality, 10*(1), 30–43. https://doi.org/10.1037/rel0000104

Neff, K. D. (2003). Self-compassion: An alternative conceptualization of a healthy attitude toward oneself. *Self and Identity, 2*(2), 85–101. https://doi.org/10.1080/15298860309032

Neff, K. D. (2011). Self-compassion, self-esteem, and well-being. *Social and Personality Psychology Compass, 5*(1), 1–12. https://doi.org/10.1111/j.1751-9004.2010.00330.x

Neimeyer, R. A. (1998). *Lessons of loss: A guide to coping.* McGraw-Hill.

Neria, Y., Nandi, A., & Galea, S. (2008). Post-traumatic stress disorder following disasters: A systematic review. *Psychological Medicine, 38*(4), 467–480. https://doi.org/10.1017/S0033291707001353

Newman, D. B., Nezlek, J. B., & Thrash, T. M. (2018). The dynamics of searching for meaning and presence of meaning in daily life. *Journal of Personality, 86*(3), 368–379. https://doi.org/10.1111/jopy.12321

Nonnemaker, J. M., McNeely, C. A., Blum, R. W., & the National Longitudinal Study of Adolescent Health. (2003). Public and private domains of religiosity and adolescent health risk behaviors: Evidence from the National Longitudinal Study of Adolescent Health. *Social Science & Medicine, 57*(11), 2049–2054. https://doi.org/10.1016/S0277-9536(03)00096-0

O'Donohue, W., Cummings, C., & Willis, B. (2018). The frequency of false allegations of child sexual abuse: A critical review. *Journal of Child Sexual Abuse, 27*(5), 459–475. https://doi.org/10.1080/10538712. 2018.1477224

Park, C. L. (2010). Making sense of the meaning literature: An integrative review of meaning making and its effects on adjustment to stressful life events. *Psychological Bulletin, 136*(2), 257–301. https://doi.org/ 10.1037/a0018301

Pattakos, A., & Dundon, E. (2017). *Prisoners of our thoughts* (3rd ed.). Berrett-Koehler Publishers.

Pearce, H., Strelan, P., & Burns, N. R. (2018). The Barriers to Forgiveness Scale: A measure of active and reactive reasons for withholding forgiveness. *Personality and Individual Differences, 134*, 337–347. https://doi.org/10.1016/j.paid.2018.06.042

Pfaltz, M. C., Passardi, S., Auschra, B., Fares-Otero, N. E., Schnyder, U., & Peyk, P. (2019). Are you angry at me? Negative interpretations of neutral facial expressions are linked to child maltreatment but not to posttraumatic stress disorder. *European Journal of Psychotraumatology, 10*(1), 1682929. https://doi.org/10.1080/20008198. 2019.1682929

Pipe, M. E., Lamb, M. E., Orbach, Y., & Cederborg, A. C. (Eds.). (2007). *Child sexual abuse: Disclosure, delay, and denial.* Routledge. https:// doi.org/10.4324/9780203936832

Prochaska, J. O., & DiClemente, C. C. (1983). Transtheoretical therapy: Toward a more integrative model of change. *Psychotherapy: Theory, Research, & Practice, 20*(2), 161–173. https://doi.org/10.1037/ h0088487

Pruitt, L. D., & Zoellner, L. A. (2008). The impact of social support: An analogue investigation of the aftermath of trauma exposure. *Journal of Anxiety Disorders, 22*(2), 253–262. https://doi.org/10.1016/ j.janxdis.2007.02.005

Roepke, A. M., Jayawickreme, R., & Riffle, O. M. (2014). Meaning and health: A systematic review. *Applied Research in Quality of Life, 9*(4), 1055–1079. https://doi.org/10.1007/s11482-013-9288-9

Rosen, L., Runtz, M., Eadie, E. M., & Mirotchnick, C. (2020). Childhood victimization and physical health in women: The mediating role of adult attachment. *Journal of Interpersonal Violence, 35*(5–6), 1182–1205. https://doi.org/10.1177/0886260517693001

Roxberg, A., Burman, M., Guldbrand, M., Fridlund, B., & da Silva, A. B. (2010). Out of the wave: The meaning of suffering and relieved suffering for survivors of the tsunami catastrophe: An hermeneutic–phenomenological study of TV-interviews one year after the tsunami catastrophe, 2004. *Scandinavian Journal of Caring Sciences, 24*(4), 707–715. https://doi.org/10.1111/j.1471-6712.2009.00767.x

Russell, D. H. (1999). *The secret trauma: Incest in the lives of girls and women.* Basic Books.

Russell, D. W., & Cutrona, C. E. (1991). Social support, stress, and depressive symptoms among the elderly: Test of a process model. *Psychology and Aging, 6*(2), 190–201. https://doi.org/10.1037/0882-7974.6.2.190

Russo-Netzer, P. (2018). Prioritizing meaning as a pathway to meaning in life and well-being. *Journal of Happiness Studies, 20*, 1863–1891. https://doi.org/10.1007/s10902-018-0031-y

Ryff, C. D. (1989). Happiness is everything, or is it? Explorations on the meaning of psychological well-being. *Journal of Personality and Social Psychology, 57*(6), 1069–1081. https://doi.org/10.1037/0022-3514.57.6.1069

Saint Arnault, D., & Sinko, L. (2019). Hope and fulfillment after complex trauma: Using mixed methods to understand healing. *Frontiers in Psychology, 10*, 2061. https://doi.org/10.3389/fpsyg.2019.02061

Schultz, J. M. (2011). *Does forgiveness matter? A study of spiritual trans-formation among survivors of significant interpersonal offenses* (Publication No. 3473239) [Doctoral dissertation, University of Iowa]. ProQuest Dissertations and Theses Global. https://doi.org/10.17077/etd.mm3ayya7

Schultz, J. M., Tallman, B. A., & Altmaier, E. M. (2010). Pathways to post-traumatic growth: The contributions of forgiveness and importance of religion and spirituality. *Psychology of Religion and Spirituality, 2*(2), 104–114. https://doi.org/10.1037/a0018454

Seeman, T. E., Dubin, L. F., & Seeman, M. (2003). Religiosity/spirituality and health: A critical review of the evidence for biological pathways. *American Psychologist, 58*(1), 53–63. https://doi.org/10.1037/0003-066X.58.1.53

Seligman, M. E. P. (2018). PERMA and the building blocks of well-being. *The Journal of Positive Psychology, 13*(4), 333–335. https://doi.org/10.1080/17439760.2018.1437466

Seligman, M. E. P., & Csikszentmihalyi, M. (2000). Positive psychology: An introduction. *American Psychologist, 55*(1), 5–14. https://doi.org/10.1037/0003-066X.55.1.5

Serpell, L., Amey, R., & Kamboj, S. K. (2020). The role of self-compassion and self-criticism in binge eating behaviour. *Appetite, 144*, 104470. https://doi.org/10.1016/j.appet.2019.104470

Shaw, A., Joseph, S., & Linley, P. A. (2005). Religion, spirituality, and post-traumatic growth: A systematic review. *Mental Health, Religion & Culture, 8*(1), 1–11. https://doi.org/10.1080/1367467032000157981

Silver, R. L., Boon, C., & Stones, M. H. (1983). Searching for meaning in misfortune: Making sense of incest. *Journal of Social Issues, 39*(2), 81–101. https://doi.org/10.1111/j.1540-4560.1983.tb00142.x

Simon, V. A., Feiring, C., & Kobielski McElroy, S. (2010). Making meaning of traumatic events: Youths' strategies for processing childhood sexual abuse are associated with psychosocial adjustment. *Child Maltreatment, 15*(3), 229–241. https://doi.org/10.1177/1077559510370365

Snyder, C. R. (2002). Hope theory: Rainbows in the mind. *Psychological Inquiry, 13*(4), 249–275. https://doi.org/10.1207/S15327965PLI1304_01

Snyder, C. R., Harris, C., Anderson, J. R., Holleran, S. A., Irving, L. M., Sigmon, S. T., Yoshinobu, L., Gibb, J., Langelle, C., & Harney, P. (1991). The will and the ways: Development and validation of an individual-differences measure of hope. *Journal of Personality and Social Psychology, 60*(4), 570–585. https://doi.org/10.1037/0022-3514.60.4.570

Snyder, C. R., & Heinze, L. S. (2005). Forgiveness as a mediator of the relationship between PTSD and hostility in survivors of childhood abuse. *Cognition and Emotion, 19*(3), 413–431. https://doi.org/10.1080/02699930441000175

Sofka, C. J. (1999). For the butterflies I never chased, I grieve: Incorporating grief and loss issues in treatment with survivors of childhood sexual abuse. *Journal of Personal and Interpersonal Loss, 4*(2), 125–148. https://doi.org/10.1080/10811449908409722

Spinazzola, J., van der Kolk, B., & Ford, J. D. (2018). When nowhere is safe: Interpersonal trauma and attachment adversity as antecedents of posttraumatic stress disorder and developmental trauma disorder. *Journal of Traumatic Stress, 31*(5), 631–642. https://doi.org/10.1002/jts.22320

Staniloiu, A., Kordon, A., & Markowitsch, H. J. (2020). Stress- and trauma-related blockade of episodic–autobiographical memory processing. *Neuropsychologia*, *139*, 107364. https://doi.org/10.1016/j.neuropsychologia.2020.107364

Stanton, A. L., & Low, C. A. (2012). Expressing emotions in stressful contexts: Benefits, moderators, and mechanisms. *Current Directions in Psychological Science*, *21*(2), 124–128. https://doi.org/10.1177/0963721411434978

Stop Abuse Campaign. (n.d.). *The ACE Test: Adverse childhood experiences.* https://stopabusecampaign.org/what-are-adverse-childhood-experiences/take-your-ace-test/

Strauss, D. (2010). *Half a life.* Random House.

Stroebe, M., & Schut, H. (1999). The dual process model of coping with bereavement: Rationale and description. *Death Studies*, *23*(3), 197–224. https://doi.org/10.1080/074811899201046

Substance Abuse and Mental Health Services Administration. (2014). *Trauma-informed care in behavioral health services: TIP 57* (Publication No. SMA 14-4816).

Tallman, B. A., Altmaier, E. M., & Garcia, C. (2007). Finding benefit from cancer. *Journal of Counseling Psychology*, *54*(4), 481–487. https://doi.org/10.1037/0022-0167.54.4.481

Tedeschi, R. G., & Calhoun, L. G. (2004). Posttraumatic growth: Conceptual foundations and empirical evidence. *Psychological Inquiry*, *15*(1), 1–18. https://doi.org/10.1207/s15327965pli1501_01

Toussaint, L., Shields, G. S., Dorn, G., & Slavich, G. M. (2016). Effects of lifetime stress exposure on mental and physical health in young adulthood: How stress degrades and forgiveness protects health. *Journal of Health Psychology*, *21*(6), 1004–1014. https://doi.org/10.1177/1359105314544132

Toussaint, L. L., Owen, A. D., & Cheadle, A. (2012). Forgive to live: Forgiveness, health, and longevity. *Journal of Behavioral Medicine*, *35*(4), 375–386. https://doi.org/10.1007/s10865-011-9362-4

Townsend, C., Rheingold, A., & Haviland, M. L. (2016). *Estimating a child sexual abuse prevalence rate for practitioners: An updated review of child sexual abuse prevalence studies.* Darkness to Light. https://www.d2l.org/wp-content/uploads/2020/01/Updated-Prevalence-White-Paper-1-25-2016_2020.pdf van der Kolk, B. (2014). *The body keeps the score: Brain, mind, and body in the healing of trauma.* Viking Press.

Van Tongeren, D. R., Aten, J. D., McElroy, S., Davis, D. E., Shannonhouse, L., Davis, E. B., & Hook, J. N. (2019). Development and validation of a measure of spiritual fortitude. *Psychological Trauma: Theory, Research, Practice, and Policy, 11*(6), 588–596. https://doi.org/10.1037/tra0000449

Vranceanu, A. M., Hobfoll, S. E., & Johnson, R. J. (2007). Child multi-type maltreatment and associated depression and PTSD symptoms: The role of social support and stress. *Child Abuse & Neglect, 31*(1), 71–84. https://doi.org/10.1016/j.chiabu.2006.04.010

Walker, D. F., Reid, H. W., O'Neill, T., & Brown, L. (2009). Changes in personal religion/spirituality during and after childhood abuse: A review and synthesis. *Psychological Trauma: Theory, Research, Practice, and Policy, 1*(2), 130–145. https://doi.org/10.1037/a0016211

Walker-Williams, H. J., & Fouché, A. (2018). Resilience enabling processes and posttraumatic growth outcomes in a group of women survivors of childhood sexual abuse. *Health SA Gesondheid, 23,* 1134. https://doi.org/10.4102/hsag.v23i0.1134

Wang, J., Mann, F., Lloyd-Evans, B., Ma, R., & Johnson, S. (2018). Associations between loneliness and perceived social support and outcomes of mental health problems: A systematic review. *BMC Psychiatry, 18*(1), 156. https://doi.org/10.1186/s12888-018-1736-5

Werner, E. E. (1993). Risk, resilience, and recovery: Perspectives from the Kauai Longitudinal Study. *Development and Psychopathology, 5*(4), 503–515. https://doi.org/10.1017/S095457940000612X

Werner-Seidler, A., Afzali, M. H., Chapman, C., Sunderland, M., & Slade, T. (2017). The relationship between social support networks and depression in the 2007 National Survey of Mental Health and Well-being. *Social Psychiatry and Psychiatric Epidemiology, 52*(12), 1463–1473. https://doi.org/10.1007/s00127-017-1440-7

Widom, C. S., Czaja, S. J., & Dutton, M. A. (2008). Childhood victimization and lifetime revictimization. *Child Abuse & Neglect, 32*(8), 785–796. https://doi.org/10.1016/j.chiabu.2007.12.006

Winters, G. M., Colombino, N., Schaaf, S., Laake, A. L. W., Jeglic, E. L., & Calkins, C. (2020). Why do child sexual abuse victims not tell anyone about their abuse? An exploration of factors that prevent and promote disclosure. *Behavioral Sciences & the Law*, *38*(6), 586–611. https://doi.org/10.1002/bsl.2492

Wolfelt, A. D. (2006). *Companioning the bereaved*. Companion Press.

Wortmann, J. H., & Park, C. L. (2008). Religion and spirituality in adjustment following bereavement: An integrative review. *Death Studies*, *32*(8), 703–736. https://doi.org/10.1080/07481180802289507

Wright, M. O., Crawford, E., & Sebastian, K. (2007). Positive resolution of childhood sexual abuse experiences: The role of coping, benefit finding, and meaning making. *Journal of Family Violence*, *22*(7), 597–608. https://doi.org/10.1007/s10896-007-9111-1

Wusik, M. F., Smith, A. J., Jones, R. T., & Hughes, M. (2015). Dynamics among posttraumatic stress symptoms, forgiveness for the perpetrator, and posttraumatic growth following collective trauma. *Journal of Community Psychology*, *43*(4), 389–394. https://doi.org/10.1002/jcop.21686

INDEX

ABOUT THE AUTHOR

Elizabeth M. Altmaier, PhD, is professor emeritus of counseling psychology and community and behavioral health at the University of Iowa. Her research focuses on issues of trauma in experiences of interpersonal offenses and on the diagnosis and treatment of cancer and chronic pain. Her studies also highlight positive processes, such as forgiveness, posttraumatic growth, and meaning making. She has published on childhood sexual abuse within faith contexts and has authored academic books on meaning making in trauma. Postretirement, she is writing, volunteering, and advocating for mental and physical health needs for underresourced persons. Dr. Altmaier lives in Iowa City.